JANICE MORPHET

BEYOND BREXIT?

How to assess the UK's future

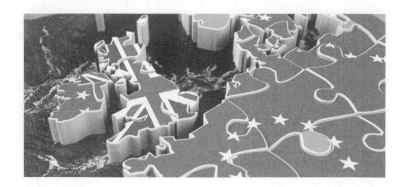

POLICY PRESS SHORTS INSIGHTS

First published in Great Britain in 2017 by

Policy Press
University of Bristol
1-9 Old Park Hill
Bristol
BS2 8BB
UK
t: +44 (0)117 954 5940
pp-info@bristol.ac.uk
www.policypress.co.uk

North America office:
Policy Press
c/o The University of Chicago Press
1427 East 60th Street
Chicago, IL 60637, USA
t: +1 773 702 7700
f: +1 773 702 9756
sales@press.uchicago.edu
www.press.uchicago.edu

© Policy Press 2017

British Library Cataloguing in Publication Data
A catalogue record for this book is available from the British Library.

Library of Congress Cataloging-in-Publication Data
A catalog record for this book has been requested.

ISBN 978-1-4473-3924-3 (paperback)
ISBN 978-1-4473-3926-7 (ePub)
ISBN 978-1-4473-3927-4 (Mobi)
ISBN 978-1-4473-3925-0 (ePDF)

Cover design by Policy Press
Front cover: image kindly supplied by Alamy
Printed and bound in Great Britain by Clays Ltd, St Ives plc
Policy Press uses environmentally responsible print partners

MIX
Paper from
responsible sources
FSC® C018072

Contents

Acknowledgements

I would like to thank Emily Watt for inviting me to consider writing this Policy Press short and also to Alison Shaw for seizing on a question asked at a seminar to invite me to write *How Europe shapes British public policy*. Thanks also go to all the other Policy Press team who are great to work with in the process of producing a book. This book also could not have been written without the many opportunities over 35 years to write and speak about the UK and the EU from the early regular EU column in *Town and Country Planning* – thanks go to the editor Nick Matthews – to recent invites to speak about Brexit. All of these activities and the questions they have posed have helped to develop my thinking.

Introduction

Thinking beyond Brexit is difficult when there is no clear government strategy to deliver the Prime Minister's objectives, or plan to achieve her outcomes. Rather, each day brings another news headline, fresh resignation or unexpected implication of what is at risk for the UK. These include the union itself, the economy and the country's world standing. The daily news round is demonstrating how little everyone in the UK knows about the way in which the EU works and how the UK has operated within it. Why is this? For the whole of its 45 years of EU membership, UK representatives from Whitehall and Westminster have been leading a double life. In practical terms, a few ministers and civil servants have been engaging in policy development, agreeing legislation and implementing it.[1] However, they have been performing a different narrative in the UK, where EU agreed decisions have been clothed in prevailing political ideology, gold-plated and presented as domestic policy initiatives unbeknown even to Parliament and the wider civil service. This deafening silence has been echoed by all forms of British media unlike other countries where *Le Monde*, for example, has consistently published 2–3 long features each week indicating how EU policy discussions that are underway will operate in different parts of France.

While this has been particularly a charge against the UK, the outgoing President of the European Parliament, Martin Schulz is now

---

[1] Janice Morphet (2013) *How Europe shapes British public policy*, Bristol: Policy Press.

suggesting that this is the default mechanism for most EU heads of state taking the position that 'we have to defend the interests of our country against Europe – as if they were being attacked by Brussels'.[2] Schulz acknowledges that Brussels has lost touch with the daily reality in many member states while also recognising that in the light of current political instabilities how important it was to expand EU membership to the east.

So do we need a crystal ball to assess what might be beyond Brexit? In this book I have tried to set out what is known about what will continue and what is very likely to be lost. I have also indicated some of the policy areas where the UK will forego future initiatives that are in progress now. The loss of the EU foundational principles of cohesion and subsidiarity – promoting social, economic and territorial equity through decision-making at the lowest optimal government level taken by directly elected and democratically elected representatives – could be incalculable. The centralising forces in the UK have done much to undermine and derail these principles in practice and now, when there appears to be some progress in achieving a step change to devolved responsibilities and finance, they are likely to be lost again, elusive as ever in the British state. These principles are core to the EU's treaties and transposing legislation will not replace their defining roles in holding governments to account.

When I wrote about the UK's relationship within the EU in 2013, I called it a sectarian issue. It has always been impossible to consider the implications of EU membership and discuss them in a meaningful way. The result of Westminster and Whitehall's denial of the EU has meant that there is no common policy language, understanding of programmes or future directions. We have always been encouraged to view the EU through a British lens, where policy is made in five year electoral cycles, in an episodic way. In the EU, policy flows in a continuous and cumulative form, in seven year delivery programmes and long time horizons. The UK has never culturally adjusted to its

---

[2]   www.theguardian.com/world/2017/jan/05/martin-schulz-eu-hamstrung-brexit-rise-populist-right?

membership, as a senior partner in a large group, instead retaining its former perceived role as a mercantile individualist nation, conquering rather than negotiating.

All of these attitudes, lack of knowledge or acknowledgement of complex policy layers that have been transcribed into individual UK initiatives are now coming to haunt these Brexit negotiations. Asking questions about specific elements that need to be considered is regarded as inconvenient and met with exasperated and consistent vilification that is little short of bullying. There is a danger that in this context, questioners fall silent, fearful of what the consequences may be for their jobs or in their communities. This book cannot provide all the questions and does not offer the answers – that is for the reader to decide what they prefer – but it starts to set out the areas where questions need to be asked and answers given. These are not one-dimensional issues but interconnected and these consequences need to be discussed. This book provides an introduction to this way of thinking about what life in the UK could be like beyond Brexit.

My hope is that through this Brexit process we are all better informed about what is to be gained and what lost. As Oscar Wilde said, a cynic is a man who knows the price of everything and the value of nothing – there is no relationship between cost and price, as the UK may be about to find out.

ONE

Brexit:
how did we get here?

Beyond Brexit?

The result of the referendum on the UK's future membership of the European Union (EU) held on 23 June 2016 can be discussed and explained in hindsight. Understanding the provenance of the vote, including the public's mood, is important, particularly in attempting to consider what might happen next both in the UK and the EU beyond Brexit. Through a discussion of the many issues swirling around and influencing this public debate, its accompanying political rhetoric and behind the scenes discussion, this book intends to provide a framework within which these developing situations can be located and considered.

'Brexit means Brexit' is a hollow mantra and as discussions continue on what it might mean more exactly for the UK, whether this is the Prime Minister's 'hard' Brexit or a 'soft' Brexit or somewhere on the continuum between them. The Brexit debate will also be influenced by the dynamic context of the politics of the United States. Citizens in the UK now find themselves knowing a lot more about the EU and the UK's agreements within its membership than they ever did before the referendum. Each day brings some new nuance or undiscovered issue that will be irrevocably influenced by Brexit and projections and disputations about its medium- and long-term economic effects on the UK.

While some parts of the media and politicians are adamant that they know what the referendum means for the future of the UK outside the EU, many more people are bewildered about what is likely to happen next, what it will mean for their lives and their jobs. These pro-Brexit politicians are full of certainty, arguing that their positive but unsecured expectations for the future are bolstered by a popularist movement sweeping across western democracies. However, not wanting to leave anything to chance, they also serve to reinforce their case through press leaks, bullying language and an emotive style that brooks no opposition or debate. Experts are dismissed as a wealthy pro-Brexit elite putting their ideology before wider consideration of their country's welfare, epitomising the London arrogance that the popular voters were so angry about. Those who favoured remain have been demonised as 'bad losers' and in denial at the result of the referendum when they ask questions or raise issues about the UK's future and how all this is to be put into effect. In this febrile environment, how is anyone able to assess what kind of negotiations the UK should be entering into with the EU when Article 50 is triggered by Parliament? How do they assess the implications of the UK's position and the content of any EU response to it?

This debate is also framed by the moral questions about implementing a non-binding referendum that expressed a majority for leaving the EU. Those in Parliament, where the remain group were in a much larger majority, are uncertain about going against the will of the people expressed in the referendum and also, for the majority of MPs, the views of their constituents. The risk of de-selection or loss of their parliamentary seat at the next general election also plays a role in these considerations. However, during the referendum campaign, the leave supporters made many claims about how the UK's contributions to the EU could be immediately switched to the NHS, only to see the slide in the value of the pound together with gloomy long-term economic projections wipe out any gains from non-payment of contributions

since the referendum. The debate about European migrants working or studying in the UK has given voice to race hate abuse and attacks, which have risen on an unprecedented scale. UK residents from the Indian sub-continent, who were encouraged to believe that voting for Brexit would bring an end to free movement of labour from the EU and would lead to more visas for their family and friends, have had their hopes dashed by the Prime Minister in an early visit to India.

This book does not provide the answers to these questions – it is for the readers and the UK electorate to assess what is on offer as the negotiations continue. However, it does try to set out the implications of some of the options that are likely to be on offer throughout the negotiations. While it seems unlikely that there will be another public vote or referendum on any proposed new arrangements between the UK and the EU, this position is now gaining ground. The proposed UK/EU agreement could also form part of the general election debate and subsequent government mandate, whether this election is held at the end of the fixed Parliament term in 2020 or before, should a political crisis arise.

Each chapter of the book is framed as a response to the question in its title and all chapters contribute to a framework to enable some appreciation not only of the specific elements of any proposed new arrangements but also some indication of the wider consequences and the interactions between these issues. It also sets out some of the choices that are available even if these are not discussed directly in the public debate on the negotiations. The last chapter draws these together to identify some of the continuing major issues that will face the UK and the EU beyond Brexit.

The road to the referendum

The referendum on the UK's membership of the EU on 23 June was held as a means to resolve a longstanding political argument within the Conservative Party. While the referendum period was quite short, from its announcement on 18 February to the referendum on 23 June, the pressure for a UK split from the EU had been growing within the

Conservative Party since the mid-1980s. The UK's membership of the EU, as set out in the European Communities Act 1972, inevitably meant the loss of some parliamentary sovereignty as laws were made by the UK with the other member states in the EU.[3] While Margaret Thatcher was recognised as being against EU membership when Prime Minister, she was always very assiduous in understanding how she could promote the UK's position within the legal frameworks of the EU and the personalities that she found herself facing around the table.[4] It was in this way that she managed her campaign for a rebate on UK contributions in 1984. It was one of the ironies of her political career that the vote to oust her as leader of the Conservative Party and Prime Minister occurred when she was in Paris.

However, despite Thatcher's rhetoric and aggressive outward stance, there were those from the UK who were working within the EU. Lord Cockfield, a former government junior minister, was responsible for developing the EU's single internal market from 1985 to its implementation in 1992. However, he found that Thatcher did not read her briefings or really engage with what was intended in the creation of the market.[5] He was critical of her lack of attention to detail and understanding of the potential advantages that the single market provided for the UK economy. This UK leadership in the development of the single market was also important for the EU. Jacques Delors, then President of the European Commission (EC), was concerned about bringing more competitiveness to the EU member state economies, making them more successful in global markets.[6] He was also keen to make the EU an economic rival to the US. He knew that the UK took a more entrepreneurial approach to economic policy than other member states and, in Delors' view, the UK's leadership of

[3] House of Commons Library (2016) 'Legislating for Brexit: the Great Repeal Bill', 21 November, http://researchbriefings.parliament.uk/ResearchBriefing/Summary/CBP-7793

[4] Thatcher, M. (1995) *The Downing Street Years*, London: Harper Collins.

[5] Cockfield, A. (1994) *The European Union*, London: John Wiley.

[6] Grant, C. (1994) *Delors: Inside The House That Jacques Built*, London: Nicholas Brealey Publishing.

the formation of the single market would provide the backing that he needed against other member states with more protectionist cultures in their trading practices.

Delors was also keen to ensure that the UK was tied more centrally into the EU as this enhanced its world standing. The UK was a member of the UN Security Council, a leading member of other global institutions and closer than other EU member states to the United States, particularly during the Reagan era. This became more important following the fall of the Berlin Wall. Delors, together with John Major, the UK Prime Minister who took over from Margaret Thatcher, developed a new role for the EU. 1992 was a random date for implementing the single market with perhaps no other significance except that it coincided with the UK's turn in chairing the EU's Council of Ministers. It allowed for the extension of the practical operation of the single market to include employment law and other issues such as free movement for workers across EU boundaries. This timing and common purpose gave the Major–Delors partnership the opportunity to create a new European Union in the form of an economic community. It provided further support for the Euro (introduced in 1995), the Schengen agreement (agreed in 1985), and an EU flag and anthem, together with an expansion to include the eastern European states.

Although the single market was important and long anticipated, the opportunity created by the eastern expansion was less expected. Together, John Major and Jacques Delors created a new approach to the whole of the EU through the Treaty for the European Union (TFEU), more frequently known as the Maastricht Treaty. This Treaty established the EU in its current form. Through this, structural funds used to support cohesion and reduce economic and social inequalities were reformed in order to enable them to be used for the former eastern states that became accession states. There was a transformation of other strategic policies such as transport and energy, creating the Trans European Networks (TEN) that could link the east to the west and the north to the south across the EU's territory.

These positive working arrangements between Delors and Major and their strategic reforms were largely hidden from view in the UK where the anti-EU faction in the Conservative Party began to grow. It was antagonistic towards Major, who famously grouped them as 'the bastards'. In 1992 Major called a 'back me or sack me' election, which he won, but this did not seem to quell the antagonism towards him from the anti-EU section of his party. However, when the Labour Party won the next general election in 1997, this was decisive and the Conservative Party spent a number of years changing leaders, uncertain about its own identity. These leaders included Eurosceptics Iain Duncan Smith and Michael Howard and Europhiles William Hague and David Cameron, although neither of the latter were strong supporters of the EU compared with other members of the Conservative Party including Kenneth Clarke.

The rise of the UK Independence Party (UKIP) from its foundation in 1991 also served to cause alarm and support a shift to the right within the Conservative Party. As it gained support and eventually two MP defections, Conservative Party members were concerned about their own electability. With the support of some parts of the UK press, they pushed for the Conservative Party to be more right wing, including promoting austerity and anti-European rhetoric. When the Conservative Party returned to power, the pressure on the Prime Minister, David Cameron, to settle the matter through a long promised referendum also grew. When Cameron won the general election in 2015 with a smaller outright majority than expected, he was pressurised into agreeing that a referendum on the UK's membership of the EU should be held. Given that the UK's turn in chairing the EU Council was programmed for 2017 and the location of the two-year negotiation period that would be triggered by a Brexit result within the EU timetable of the budget and elections, and the general elections in France, Netherlands and Germany in 2017, the optimal timing of the UK's referendum on EU membership was in the first half of 2016. As with all EU matters, the timing is critical.[7]

The Conservative Party was split in the referendum campaign with key members of the party and government supporting the leave side. When the results were known, David Cameron resigned as Prime Minister the following day and, following a leadership process for the new Conservative Party leader and Prime Minister, Theresa May, who was a marginal remain supporter for defence and security reasons, was appointed as eventually the only candidate left standing. The new Prime Minister appointed three leading 'leave' members of the Conservative Party to her new Cabinet to lead the Brexit negotiations, to develop new international trade and as Foreign Secretary.

However, despite all this, the 'leave' group has continued its campaign through attacks on the new Chancellor of the Exchequer and the Governor of the Bank of England while seemingly forcing the UK's EU Ambassador to resign. When the government lost its challenge and subsequent appeal in the courts on the way in which Article 50 is to be triggered, determining that power to take the decision lay with Parliament rather than with the government through its proposed use of the royal prerogative, the pro-'leave' press and members of the Conservative Party then attacked the judiciary in a way that is unprecedented in the UK. The pro-'leave' campaigners have increasingly marked their campaigns by personal attacks on individuals in a threatening manner and do not seem to understand or accept the UK's constitution. There has also been a flexible relationship with facts that have set the debates within a 'post-truth' context.

Those in favour of remain appear be disorganised and still in shock while these repeated forms of incursion into government and constitutional conventions continue. The 2016 leadership contest in the Labour Party was marked by the same division between those in favour of ideology through post-truth disruption and the rest of

[7]   Morphet, J. (2013) *How Europe shapes British public policy*, Bristol: Policy Press; Goetz, Klaus H. and Meyer-Sahling, Jan-Hinrik (eds) (2012) *The EU Timescape*, London: Routledge.

the party. Meanwhile, UKIP, having achieved its objective, has had difficulty appointing a new leader and has been riven by internal division.

Brief context on the UK's relationship with the EU

The UK has always had a difficult relationship with the EU compared with other member states.[8] This has been rooted in a different conception of the EU, whereby those in Westminster and particularly in Whitehall have had an arm's length approach,[9] treating agreements made with other member states as being less binding than their legal status requires. While the European Communities Act 1972 stated that European law would be sovereign in the EU's areas of competence this has never been accepted in practice,[10] to the point of denial. The physical separation of the UK and the member states on the European mainland has always served to reinforce this institutional distance. The high proportion of land borders on mainland Europe between member states has emphasised the issues about the costs and inefficiencies of these borders for the movement of people and goods. Moreover, the experience of two world wars has brought different sensibility to the culture and politics of much of the creation of the EU. Mainland Europe has also been more welfarist in its culture and supportive of its citizens. It has been against liberalisation of labour markets and in favour of support for working people through trade unions and state supported services. There has also been a strong culture of purchasing goods from domestic markets rather than making these markets open more widely. The advent of more globalisation has not been so widely espoused as in the UK and the US, and in France, the EU is regarded as the 'wooden horse' of market liberalism.

---

[8] Chadha, J. (2016) 'UK and Europe: what next?' *National Institute Economic Review*, no 236, November, pp 1–3.

[9] Burch, M. and Bulmer, S. (2008) *The Europeanisation of Whitehall*, Manchester: Manchester University Press.

[10] Morphet (2013).

In comparison, the UK, as an island, has always had strong borders and has had a history of exercising hard and soft power. It does not see the EU as its main source of political influence in global affairs and exercises its own soft power through the use of its language, the royal family, legal systems, the Commonwealth and stable political system. It also exercises hard power and influence through its active commitment to defence and security policy, a seat on the UN Security Council, membership of the G7 and G20, its diplomatic service and as a founder of international bodies. While the combined EU economy is larger than that of the US, on the day of the referendum the UK had the fifth largest global economy, second to Germany in the EU. The parliamentary system in the UK has also been copied by many countries and, following the end of the Second World War in 1945, the UK was a contributor to the establishment of the form of the German state and constitution.

The UK's views on membership of the EU, when it was formed, were fraught with an initial arrogance and complacency about its function and role. In 1963, the US, through President Kennedy, finally persuaded the UK to join the EU, through Prime Minister Macmillan, his cousin. The US, understanding the economic and political potential and ambition of this new group, preferred the UK inside the EU to exert influence rather than remaining outside. The UK then began to pursue membership with more vigour, although it was met by the resistance of one of its former allies, General de Gaulle in France. The long delay in the UK's recognition of the future power of the EU and its need for membership related not only to its role in two world wars but also its colonial past where it had not developed any cultural practices of sharing power or joint working.[11]

The debates about EU membership in the Houses of Parliament were initially open about the loss of sovereignty over legislation in those areas that the UK pooled with the EU but when this aroused some

---

[11] Mount, Ferdinand (2016) 'Nigels against the world', *London Review of Books*, 19 May, vol 38, no 10, pp 21–3, www.lrb.co.uk/v38/n10/ferdinand-mount/nigels-against-the-world

questions and opposition, it was quietly dropped from the debate. Since this point, there has been no discussion about the role of the decisions that the UK makes within the EU and how these are implemented. Parliamentary statements of EU Council meetings attended by government ministers are made without the word 'Europe' in their headers and reports of these meetings on the floor of the Houses of Parliament are made minimal and frequently with no mention of the significant issues discussed or agreed. Parliamentary scrutiny of any EU matters has been fragmented and not reported clearly. The civil service has continued to fail to grasp and embrace the relationship and has been resistant to implementing agreements made by the UK in the EU. The civil service has not actively encouraged its own members to gain experience in the EC as part of their personal training and development, unlike other member states.

Despite being a member for over 40 years, there is very little public knowledge and familiarity of how the EU works, the meetings that are held and the decisions that are made, as became abundantly clear in discussions on the radio and television during the period before the referendum. For most of the period of the UK's membership of the EU, decisions and legislation have been clothed in a UK wrapper and it is only since the referendum was called that EU policies and legislation in the UK are being made available in their original form.

The position in Scotland, Wales and Northern Ireland has been more informed. This is partly because these nations have received more funding from the EU given their economic and social wellbeing status and the differences between their economies and the UK average. They also have more interest in the EU as their own pressure for independence and nationhood is supported by the EU principle of subsidiarity. In Northern Ireland the Good Friday Agreement, supported by the EU, the culmination of the peace process, has been a key factor in supporting change.

What is Article 50?

The process through which the UK will negotiate any departure from the EU is set out in Article 50 of the Lisbon Treaty 2007.[12] Before this, there were no provisions for any member state to leave the EU, although this would have been possible under the conventions of international law. As with many other ironies in the relationship between the UK and EU, Article 50 was drafted by Lord Kerr, former head of the UK's diplomatic service and former UK ambassador to the EU.

Article 50 does not set out any substantive conditions that would require a member state to leave the EU but rather procedural requirements if it is invoked voluntarily. The consequences of any member state withdrawing from the EU means an end to the application of the EU treaties and of EU law in that state. Any presentation of EU law is always anchored in the treaty from which it takes its *vires*. These treaties act as a constitutional basis for all subsequent decisions and case law. Article 50 provides for a member state on leaving to transpose EU law into its domestic law, which would then be effective until the state decides to amend or repeal it. The Article also states that it will be a consideration of the effect that the removal of legislation will have on the longer term relationship that the withdrawing state wants to have with the EU. Thus the continuing use of legislation and its operation will be in the context of the negotiated relationship between the leaving state and the EU.

The process of withdrawal from the EU depends on the member state notifying the European Council that it wishes to withdraw. Following negotiations that can include the future relationship with the EU, it will be concluded by a super qualified majority vote in the European Council after obtaining consent from the European Parliament. The European Parliament can withhold agreement of

---

[12] European Parliament (2016) 'Briefing: Article 50 TEU: Withdrawal of a Member State from the EU', February, www.europarl.europa.eu/RegData/etudes/BRIE/2016/577971/EPRS_BRI(2016)577971_EN.pdf

any proposed negotiated settlement. The European Council majority would need to be at least 72% of the members representing at least 65% of the population of the EU, with the exception of the member state wishing to withdraw. The agreement does not need to be ratified by all the member states, but this will be the case if there are subsequent agreements on free trade, the continued access to the European Investment Bank or other international agreements either agreed as part of the Article 50 process or subsequently. The form of the legal arrangements following the departure of a member state requires that all EU treaties will need to be amended to remove references to the former member and this may open up the possibility of renegotiation on other issues within remaining EU member states.[13]

For the member state invoking the Article 50 process, EU legislation will cease to apply after two years although this period can be extended by the agreement of both parties. If a member state leaves the EU, it can apply to rejoin under the terms of Article 49. Also, although the issue of Article 50 proceedings cannot be revoked,[14] it can be suspended if all parties agree. There has also been consideration of a partial withdrawal from the EU but this could be achieved through renegotiation of the treaties rather than triggering Article 50. Another issue arises if parts of a member state wish to remain after a member state has concluded terms to leave the EU. The view here is that this part of the state is not a sovereign state and so cannot remain in membership. In Scotland, the First Minister has argued that should Scotland vote for independence and become a sovereign state, then it could become the legal successor state to the UK, although this is disputed. In this case an independent Scotland could apply to join the EU using Article 49. This issue is likely to be resolved practically within

---

[13] Lazowski, A. (2012) 'Withdrawal from the European Union and alternatives to membership', *European Law Review*, vol 37, no 5, pp 523–40.

[14] The issue of revocation is a vexed one legally and there are differing views on it. See Oxford Human Rights Hub (2016) 'Brexit: Foundational Constitutional and Interpretative Principles: II', 28 October, http://ohrh.law.ox.ac.uk/brexit-foundational-constitutional-and-interpretive-principles-ii/

the EU, as occurred when Czechoslovakia split into two countries and Germany reunified.

Following the referendum there has been debate about how and when Article 50 will be triggered. The timing question was answered by the Prime Minister at the Conservative Party conference when she confirmed that this would be before the end of March 2017.[15] There have been a number of discussions about the best time to trigger Article 50 given other events occurring in the EU during 2017 including the French, Dutch and German general elections. There have been arguments to suggest that it would be better to wait until the end of 2017 before triggering Article 50 when there would be a better understanding of the likely negotiation position and its nuances.[16] Also it would recognise that, once Article 50 has been triggered, there will be a series of discussions and meetings to determine the EU's negotiating position on any UK requests for associated negotiations as permitted in the Article.

A much greater debate has been held on how Article 50 could be triggered. The government has argued that the referendum result allows it to exercise the royal prerogative to trigger Article 50 as an executive action without the need to take the issue to Parliament for a vote. This position has been challenged by the First Ministers of Scotland and Wales, who have argued that under the devolved settlement and their foundational legislation they need to be included in the decision making. It has also been challenged through the courts. In Northern Ireland two cases were brought about the need to have a parliamentary debate given that Northern Ireland did not vote to leave the EU. There have been other similar cases in England.

---

[15] 'Theresa May's keynote speech at Tory conference in full', 5 October 2016, www.independent.co.uk/news/uk/politics/theresa-may-speech-tory-conference-2016-in-full-transcript-a7346171.html

[16] Kaivanto, K. (2016) 'Not being smart about Article 50: the strategic considerations of an early 2017 notification', 3 October, http://blogs.lse.ac.uk/politicsandpolicy/not-being-smart-about-article-50-the-strategic-considerations-of-an-early-2017-notification/

A second set of cases has been brought before the High Court, arguing that as the European Communities Act 1972 put EU law into domestic law, triggering Article 50, with no revocation rights, would lead to a loss of citizen rights as a consequence. As noted earlier, the Article 50 process can be paused by agreement of both the member state and the EU but there is no automatic right to this agreement. It was claimed in the challenge in the High Court that it was therefore for Parliament to vote on invoking Article 50. The High Court, sitting with the most senior three judges in England and Wales, found that in the matter of the constitution, the government could not exercise the royal prerogative in issuing Article 50, and had to take the matter before Parliament to agree it. On the day of the judgement, 3 November 2016, the government announced that it would appeal this decision and that this case would be heard in the Supreme Court by 11 judges that would sit in early December. In January, the Supreme Court found against the government stating that to proceed otherwise would be a breach of settled constitutional principles stretching back many centuries.

The governments in Scotland and Wales applied to join the defendants in this case and also to raise the constitutional issues about the effects of the referendum on their constitutional position. The Supreme Court gave Scotland and Wales permission to join this case and bring their additional specific arguments. In their outline statement of case, both governments have disputed the rights of the government to take decisions on the UK's EU membership by determining that it is a non-devolved matter of foreign and international policy.[17] The outline case also reminds the court of the terms of the legislative consent principle and legislation between Scotland and the UK Parliament which prohibits the UK Parliament from legislating on any matter affecting Scotland without agreement from the Scottish

[17] BBC News (2016) 'Lord Advocate calls for Holyrood consent over Brexit', 25 November, www.bbc.co.uk/news/uk-scotland-scotland-politics-38110677; Institute for Government (2016) 'Four-nation Brexit', Briefing Paper, www.instituteforgovernment.org.uk/publications/four-nation-brexit

Parliament. The case was not found for Scotland and Wales so this brings forward the potential for another independence referendum in Scotland.

The Government subsequently presented a Bill to parliament on 26 January while the Prime Minister also agreed to publish an accompanying White paper.[18] On 4 November 2016, the Prime Minister assured the President of the EC that she intended to adhere to the deadline that she had set of triggering Article 50, 31 March 2017.

Parliament's role in the Brexit process is important, not least as it could tie the government's hands in negotiation. The government has consistently argued that Parliament's involvement would be unnecessary although this position appears less credible as more discussion ensues on the range of options available for the UK/EU relationships after Brexit. It has also been argued that Parliament may refuse to invoke Article 50. In this case it would still be open to Parliament to mandate the government to negotiate some other form of relationship that might include differential arrangements for the devolved nations and London. Brexit supporters have argued that this would be an undemocratic move for Parliament to make. However, the UK's referendum on EU membership was not legally binding on Parliament, although those in favour of leaving the EU argue that it is morally binding and this is the position taken by most MPs at present. However, the arguments for remain have been fuelled by the economic and financial forecasts in the 2016 Autumn Statement on the future position of the UK economy together with the commentary of the Office of Budget Responsibility, set up to examine government financial and economic policy, and the Institute for Fiscal Studies.[19]

There are also other dynamic political events that may provide some influence on the debate to be held by Parliament whether this is on

[18] www.gov.uk/government/uploads/system/uploads/attachment_data/file/589191/The_United_Kingdoms_exit_from_and_partnership_with_the_EU_Web.pdf

[19] Walker, P. and Elgot, J. (2016) 'Bid to challenge Brexit gathers pace among pro-remain politicians', *Guardian*, 26 November, www.theguardian.com/politics/2016/nov/26/bid-to-challenge-brexit-gathers-pace-among-pro-remain-politicians

the point of invoking Article 50 or later. These include the election of the new US president – Donald Trump – and his likely economic and foreign policies, which are yet to be fully unveiled. The EU may also choose to take other positions as the leadership campaigns in the French elections are expecting to be focused on the likely influence of Brexit and Trump on domestic policy. The EU may decide to take some specific actions on free trade and globalisation if, as expected, the new US administration abandons the Transatlantic Trade and Investment Partnership (TTIP) agreement that has been developed between the US and the EU. It may also move the EU to give more power to the European Parliament as the only directly elected institution within the EU. All of this will contribute to the fluidity of the Article 50 negotiations and the extent to which the EU and UK move their positions in the light of a cooler global political climate operating on more protectionist principles.

Implications of the referendum for Scotland, Northern Ireland, Wales and Gibraltar

The implications for the nations of the UK with their own Parliaments and Assemblies and Gibraltar are each different although there are some aspects of their position which are common. For Scotland, Wales and Northern Ireland and to some extent London, UK membership of the EU is a fundamental component of their devolved powers: the devolution of many powers from the UK government to devolved national Parliaments derive from the legislation that the UK has already agreed within the EU.[20] Hence devolution is not about basic powers but rather about the choice in the means of implementation of EU legislation already agreed.[21] There are some exceptions to this such as primary and secondary education but even these issues are covered by EU legislation on the applicability of World Trade Organization

---

[20] Scottish Government (2016) *Scotland: A European Nation*, www.gov.scot/ Publications/2016/11/4961
[21] Morphet (2013).

(WTO) rules on competition for public services. The major issues for Scotland, Northern Ireland and Wales if the UK leaves the EU will be to what extent they will retain their existing powers of decision making over the implementation of legislation or whether a new set of powers will need to be identified.

Further, would this need to be set out in a federal constitution in the UK that would guarantee devolution that is currently secured through subsidiarity principles enshrined in EU treaties? Devolution within the UK has been supported through the application of the principle of subsidiarity that was part of the Treaty of Rome but has since been developed in the TFEU 1992 and the Lisbon Treaty 2007. This approach to subsidiarity has been supported by the OECD, which is a membership organisation with influential, but soft, power and no means of legal enforcement. If the UK leaves the EU without replacing this principle of subsidiarity that is in the foundational treaties of the EU, then the position of Scotland, Wales and Northern Ireland together with London and the combined authorities in England may be more tenuous and there may be some pressure to return powers to central government.

UK Devolution and the British-Irish Council

The engagement of the UK nations and London in Article 50 negotiations with the UK government had a slippery start. Following devolution in Scotland and Wales in 1999, a joint memorandum of understanding was agreed that allows for consultation and sharing of information. The Joint Ministerial Committee (JMC) was established. The Institute for Government explains how this relationship works:

> On EU business, the four governments engage through a sub-committee of this main Joint Ministerial Committee. This body – the Joint Ministerial Committee on Europe (JMCE) – has typically met several times a year since 1999, usually in advance of European Council meetings. The committee, chaired by the UK Foreign Secretary, gives devolved administrations the

opportunity to voice their views and raise concerns about EU policy issues that are being negotiated in Brussels, and on which the UK has to take a unified position.[22]

However, the JMCE is not seen as the location for discussions about Brexit as it has traditionally acted as an advisory committee to the UK government which has set the agenda and made subsequent decisions without the need for examination or to report back.

Since the Good Friday Agreement in 1998, the nations of the UK together with Ireland, the States of Jersey and Guernsey and the Isle of Man have been meeting regularly as the British–Irish Council (BIC). The BIC had a temporary secretariat but this was made permanent in 2012 and is located in Edinburgh. The BIC has more relevance to all its members with the possible exception of England, which is represented by the UK around the table. The BIC has a range of working groups that are proposed by ministers from any member state and their work is then reported back to a meeting of the BIC.[23]

Following the result of the UK referendum on membership of the EU, a special meeting of the BIC was called in Cardiff to discuss the issues for devolution for devolved nations. The BIC members agreed to request full inclusion in the negotiations and subsequent settlements although no clear legal pathway has been established. Although the BIC exists to discuss matters within the UK, the Prime Minister has chosen to establish a specific committee to work with the Secretary of State for Exiting the European Union, David Davis. The Institute for Government (2016) had argued that:

the Governments should also agree how each will be involved at crucial stages of the Brexit process, such as agreeing the final deal. These words should be followed up with action, for example,

---

[22] Institute for Government (2016).

[23] Morphet, J. and Clifford, B. (2016) "Who else would we speak to?' National Policy Networks in post-devolution Britain: The case of spatial planning', *Public Policy and Administration*, 3 October, 0952076716669978.

publication of agreed principles for co-operation, including what issues are on the table and how disputes between the four nations will be resolved.[24]

It also comments that 'Failure to do this now risks seriously damaging relations between the four governments'. The Secretary of State for Brexit will also have weekly meetings with the Mayor of London.

Scotland

The position of Scotland in relation to the UK referendum on EU membership is set within the context of the referendum that was held on Scottish independence in 2014. In that referendum, the arguments in favour of Scotland remaining within the UK were said to be influenced by the UK's membership of the EU. This position appeared to be less certain for immediate EU membership if Scotland voted to become independent from the UK.

This position has changed since the UK referendum on EU membership. Scotland voted 62% to remain in the EU and as a country was against leaving. The First Minister Nicola Surgeon has argued that Scotland's position should be recognised in the negotiations after Article 50 has been invoked. The First Minister has also stated that Scotland should come to some arrangement that would allow continuing membership. The Prime Minister has sounded more sympathetic on this issue than her ministers in the government responsible for Article 50 negotiations who have maintained a centralised and non-devolved UK view of decision making and negotiation. The First Minister has appointed a Minister responsible for Brexit and also strengthened policy teams working on Scotland–EU issues. She has also appointed an expert advisory group.

---

[24] Munro, R. (2016) 'What the Government needs to demonstrate before it pulls the Article 50 trigger', Institute for Government blog, 27 October, www.instituteforgovernment.org.uk/blog/14819/what-the-government-needs-to-demonstrate-before-it-pulls-the-article-50-trigger

The First Minister has also been exploring the mechanisms through which continuing Scotland–EU relations can be maintained and in October 2016 stated that this might mean a second independence referendum. In this case, if Scotland voted for independence then Scotland could apply to be the UK's successor nation and remain in the EU without applying for membership. If Scotland becomes independent and applies for membership of the EU it will be obliged to go through accession processes in Article 49, which should be relatively easy for compliance, but there may be issues where the UK has had a specific agreement that may not apply in a new membership application. These include membership of the Schengen agreement for free movement of people and of the Eurozone.

The verdict of the High Court about Parliament's role in triggering the submission of procedures under Article 50 has also caused some rethinking in Scotland and the First Minister decided that Scotland should join with the defendants at the appeal by government to the Supreme Court concerning the dispute between the role of the executive and Parliament in invoking Article 50.

There would be advantages for Scotland to remain or become a member of the EU if the rest of the UK exits. These are primarily related to its potential location for the financial services industry that would need to be within the EU for 'passporting' purposes. Edinburgh has been the location of finance industries for many years and Edinburgh may be considered a more attractive location for financial services staff in comparison to other locations such as Dublin and Frankfurt.

Northern Ireland

Northern Ireland has been in receipt of support funding from the EU since 1989 through a successive range of programmes, labelled PEACE since 1995. The purpose of these programmes has been to support cohesion between communities involved in the conflict in Northern Ireland and the border counties of Ireland and economic and social stability.

The position of Northern Ireland in relation to the result of the UK's referendum on membership of the EU is particularly difficult when Northern Ireland voted to remain. In Northern Ireland the work on Brexit is led by the Executive Office, which is the joint office that supports the First and the Deputy First Ministers. The specific challenges for Northern Ireland that relate to the EU are two-fold. On the assumption that Scotland remains within the UK, then Northern Ireland will have the only land border that the UK has with the EU. This is a rural border that is porous and has been difficult to secure at times of internal tensions in the island of Ireland. This land border is associated with the agreements made at the establishment of the Irish Free State and the common travel area (CTA). There may also be additional issues that relate to entry to the UK via this land border and there have already been suggestions that passport control for EU citizens should be for the whole of the island of Ireland rather than just through Northern Ireland. This is difficult and might damage Ireland's relationship with the EU.

The second issue is the basis of the peace process and the 1998 Good Friday Agreement, which is based on EU law. Since 1998, the establishment of the Northern Ireland Assembly and subsequent devolution of powers has been founded on this agreement and its signatories remain the UK, Ireland, the EU and the US. There have been some comments that the withdrawal of the UK from the EU would fundamentally change the terms of the Good Friday Agreement of which the EU is a signatory.

Any Article 50 negotiations would need to consider both of these issues and how they will be dealt with in future. There have already been calls for the island of Ireland to be politically reunified and for Northern Ireland to leave the UK. Although there was a majority in favour of remain in the EU in Northern Ireland there is a political and sectarian spilt, with many Unionist party supporters voting to leave the EU. This matter appears to be further complicated by the High Court's decisions that Parliament should be involved in triggering Article 50 and may mean that Sinn Fein MPs take up their seats in the UK Parliament for the first time in order to vote on this issue.

There have also been considerable concerns from the Republic of Ireland and whole island discussions are being held to consider ways in which the future can be managed. When the UK joined the EU in 1972, Ireland also joined as its currency was linked to sterling and most of its trade with the UK. Now Ireland has become a strong member of the EU but it remains concerned that the withdrawal of the UK from membership could increase its peripherality and also remove one of its allies from the EU. The Prime Minister of the UK has reassured Ireland that there will be no hard land borders between the north and south and that the Common Movement Area would remain. US Senator George Mitchell, who negotiated the Good Friday Agreement, has stated that any reintroduction of a land border between Northern Ireland and Ireland would be a very retrogressive step.[25] The EU's lead negotiator on Brexit, Michel Barnier, was also a member of the team that negotiated this agreement and is well acquainted with these issues.

Wales

The people of Wales voted against remaining in the EU in the UK referendum on EU membership. In Wales, the First Minister, Carwyn Jones, is leading on Brexit with strong support from the Finance Minister and he has also established an expert advisory body to assist in the work. The First Minister has stated that the Welsh government will abide by this decision and support Brexit although there are concerns for the future of rural policy and structural funds support, particularly for those parts of Wales where the economy is much below national and European averages. Wales might particularly suffer from the move away from the Common Agricultural Policy as the UK would then be obliged to operate under the WTO agreements for agriculture without the benefit of the additional agreement that

[25] BBC News (2016) 'Border controls 'a step backwards' warns US senator George Mitchell', 30 October, www.bbc.co.uk/news/uk-northern-ireland-37811410

the EU has negotiated with the WTO for rural land management subsidies. Elsewhere, parts of Wales benefit from structural funds that would no longer be available after Brexit. The UK government initially declined to confirm if these structural funds would be available after Brexit but has subsequently confirmed that projects commenced by 23 November 2016 would be assured of their funding until 2020. This has subsequently been extended until the point that the UK leaves the EU. Wales was also on the path of achieving more devolution but recent manoeuvres by Whitehall around the Wales Bill 2016 suggest that some powers devolved in earlier legislation are being removed and returned to Whitehall.

Gibraltar

Gibraltar is a British Overseas territory and its links with the UK rest in the 1713 Treaty of Utrecht, which states that if the UK gives up Gibraltar then Spain has the first rights on it. Although Gibraltar became part of the EU as an overseas territory when the UK joined the EU in 1972, its citizens were not able to vote in European Parliament elections until 2004 when it joined the South West England constituency.

In the UK referendum Gibraltar voted 96% in favour of remaining in the EU. Since the referendum, the Chief Minister of the Gibraltar government has stated that it is their intention to negotiate a relationship with the EU that retains access to the EU's single market and also provides free access across its border.[26] The potential for retaining a different relationship with the rest of the EU is based on the current position of Gibraltar in relation to the customs union, which it is outside. The opening of talks with the EU could also

[26] Morales, M. (2016) 'Brexit latest: Gibraltar seeks EU deal that keeps free movement and single market', *Independent*, 27 September, www.independent.co.uk/news/business/news/brexit-latest-gibraltar-seeks-eu-deal-that-keeps-free-movement-and-single-market-a7332336.html

reopen claims by Spain on Gibraltar and this could be a bargaining pawn in the discussions.[27]

Jersey, Guernsey and the Isle of Man

Jersey is a crown dependency, although it differs in its relationship with the head of state in comparison with Guernsey and the Isle of Man. Jersey is not part of the UK but the UK has responsibility for its defence. In 2003, the EC confirmed that Jersey was part of the European territory for whose external relationships the UK is responsible. Jersey is not part of the EU but is part of the customs union with free movement of goods and people between the island and member states, although the EU rules on free movement of workers do not apply in Jersey. Jersey is not part of the single market for financial services although it is able to have access to the market through demonstrating that its rules have equivalence with EU legislation. There is now some doubt on Jersey's status in these financial arrangements in the future. Citizens of the crown dependencies were not allowed to vote in the UK referendum on EU membership. The UK's position on the relationship between these crown dependencies and Brexit has been exacerbated by the issues on tax cooperation between them and the EU.[28] All three states continue to play an active role in the BIC and the discussions of the future relationships between the members.[29]

---

[27] Henley, J. (2016) 'Rocked by Brexit vote, Gibraltar lays plans for new kind of EU relationship', *Guardian*, 22 October, www.theguardian.com/politics/2016/oct/22/gibraltar-brexit-vote-new-eu-relationship

[28] Bailiwick Express (2015) 'EU Commissioner: "Jersey is an important partner against tax evasion and fraud"', 6 May, www.bailiwickexpress.com/jsy/news/eu-commissioner-jersey-are-important-partners-against-tax-evasion-and-fraud/#.WDIps_mLTIU

[29] GOV.GG (2016) 'Guernsey attends 28th British-Irish Summit in Cardiff', 25 November, www.gov.gg/article/157134/Guernsey-attends-28th-British-Irish-Council-Summit-in-Cardiff

Post-Brexit options

There are some strong arguments for the nations of the UK to be included in Brexit discussions and negotiations. As noted above, their foundational legislation is fundamentally affected by Brexit. The Institute for Government has argued that they should be treated as partners and that:

> there should be 'parity of esteem' between the four administrations. This would not mean the four governments will be equal partners in the process, but it would involve recognition that these are four democratically elected governments working together in good faith to seek a joint approach, even if Westminster retains the power to have the final say.[30]

The Prime Minister has also confirmed that the crown dependencies will be involved in discussions about future UK arrangements with the EU.

As Chapter Three shows, there are a number of post-Brexit options for the devolved nations and Gibraltar. These include the potential for the reverse Greenland option whereby Scotland, Northern Ireland and Gibraltar remain in the EU while England and Wales leave. Another option is that parts of the UK leave and become independent states in their own right and apply for accession to the EU or, in the case of Scotland, as a potential successor state. For Gibraltar, it has been argued that the Treaty of Utrecht 1713 now no longer applies and Gibraltar's future would be considered under the principle of self-determination. This provides Gibraltar with the potential to become an independent micro state and then apply for accession or a negotiated relationship in the same way as other micro states within the EU. Duursma, a constitutional expert, has stated that:

[30] Institute for Government (2016).

Gibraltar can therefore have direct access to the EU rather than through any other country. All that is needed is for UK to authorise Gibraltar to sign direct agreements with the EU even if the UK does not do so itself. That foundation could then later be used to declare independence if Gibraltar's people want that in the future.[31]

The foreign ministers of Jersey and Guernsey have also suggested that this would be the way forward for the islands.[32] [33]

Another approach has been proposed by former Prime Minister Gordon Brown. He has suggested that the UK should hold a constitutional convention with a view to reforming the UK into a federal state with greater powers of determination over law within each nation. He has argued that would be a better reflection of both day-to-day purposes in the UK but would also be the only means of holding together the union.

Legal and constitutional issues: the known unknowns?

While some of the legal and constitutional issues that surround Brexit can be determined at this stage, as the period since the UK referendum has already demonstrated, there are more consequential unknowns and options emerging. Those who are directly affected are raising questions and others with less immediate appreciation of the issues are gradually being brought into an ever widening circle of public debate

---

[31] Gibraltar Panorama (2016) 'Utrecht is no longer valid – and Gibraltar can become a micro-state in the EU, says legal expert', 14 October, http://gibraltarpanorama.gi/15209/244313/a/utrecht-is-no-longer-valid-and-gibraltar-can-become-a-micro-state-in-the-eu-says

[32] ITV News (2016) 'Jersey could vote for independence from UK following Brexit', 27 June, www.itv.com/news/channel/update/2016-06-27/jersey-could-vote-for-independence-from-uk-following-brexit

[33] Guernsey Press (2016) 'Brexit fall-out could see island part of a union of microstates', 20 July, http://guernseypress.com/news/2016/07/20/brexit-fall-out-could-see-island-part-of-a-union-of-microstates

and comment. Some of those who voted for Brexit are wondering why it has not already happened as they were given the impression that the UK contributions to the EU could be withdrawn immediately and diverted into the NHS. There is a plethora of comment and opinion that is continuous in its form rather than being based on a two sided argument.[34] New issues are emerging all the time and these need to be discussed and then located within the context of the existing debates about principles and powers.

The House of Commons Library in Parliament has attempted to identify what it has entitled 'Brexit Unknowns'[35] that include issues of the negotiation process, the effects on the UK's trading position and how long the process will take. Although Article 50 provides for the UK to incorporate EU law into its own until it is replaced, there are numerous unknowns about how this legislation will work, how it will be transposed, and who will be responsible for interpreting it if it is challenged – currently this is the European Court of Justice.[36] Also, as noted above, all pieces of EU legislation are rooted in specific and individual treaty provisions and if the treaties are no longer operational within the UK, how will this legislation be interpreted if disputed? There will be other questions about how long this legislation will remain in place together with debates about new bases of policy other than the EU treaties for the legislation when it is replaced. The government and the EU are now recognising the need for transitional arrangements[37] although there are many questions about how these

---

[34] House of Commons Library (2016) 'Statement on Article 50: 7 November 2016', www.parliament.uk/business/news/2016/november/statement-on-article-50-7-november-2016

[35] House of Commons Library (2016) 'Brexit: some legal, constitutional and financial unknowns', 9 November, http://researchbriefings.parliament.uk/ResearchBriefing/Summary/CBP-7761

[36] House of Commons Library (2016) 'Legislating for Brexit: the Great Repeal Bill'.

[37] Mason, R. and Rankin, J. (2016) 'PM warned transition Brexit deal 'fiendishly difficult' to achieve', *Guardian*, 21 November, www.theguardian.com/politics/2016/nov/21/pm-warned-transition-brexit-deal-fiendishly-difficult-

might operate in practice. This process might also be made more complex if the UK enters into an EU trading agreement post Brexit that requires some adherence to EU legislation as a requirement.

to-achieve-theresa-may-eu; Ash, T.G. (2016) 'Soft or hard Brexit? The EU, not Britain, has the whip hand', *Guardian*, 24 November, www.theguardian. com/commentisfree/2016/nov/24/soft-hard-brexit-eu-britain-uk

TWO

What does the EU do for the UK and the UK for the EU?

Much of the debate before the referendum focused on the position of the UK as being a net contributor to the EU's finances and what that funding could be used for if it were repatriated. Brexit campaigners suggested that it could be transferred into the NHS budget. There was little wider debate about the value of the UK's membership of the EU beyond these payments and also what benefits the UK's membership brings to the EU. This chapter seeks to distinguish between the (financial) cost of the UK's membership of the EU and its (societal) price which, in the economic maxim, can frequently bear no relationship to each other. In this, the financial cost of making something or providing a service is completely detached from the price that anyone is prepared to pay for these goods or services. When the UK joined the EU, the price included subscribing to the principles of economic and social cohesion, giving up some of its sovereignty in return for trading opportunities to a tariff free market and working together on other borderless issues such as the environment. As the EU has developed its role in relation to these issues, the UK has been behind these developments, often paving the way for them to occur. Yet the UK has never owned its EU membership – always half in and half out, looking to the east and the west at the same time.

In this chapter some of the benefits of EU membership to the UK are considered. This is accompanied by a review of the benefits that the UK's membership gives to the EU. This is not a one sided picture and this discussion is intended to inform the consideration of the offer made to the UK within the negotiations after Article 50 is invoked. While the discussion on negotiation and terms may be set within the context of payments and now more frequently rights of the country to choose its own destiny, this debate can also be considered within a wider framework.

What does the EU do for the UK?

The way that the EU works is culturally and institutionally different from the UK. It is an organisation that frames its work through its legislation and powers but operates within pragmatic decision making systems. It has multiple ways of making a decision[38] from a treaty, through legislative means – regulations and directives – made by the Council of Ministers to operationalise and implement the treaties' powers. The EU has other means such as COREPER (Committee of Permanent Representatives), two groups of leading member state officials who can make decisions on behalf of their governments where there are few or no show stopping objections to a policy or action. There are also co-decision making spaces between the Council of Ministers, the European Parliament and European Commission where negotiations and trade-offs can be agreed. Beyond that, there are informal Council decisions and Ministerial groups where member states can agree to act together if there are no formal powers or there are some member state objections. Member states can work together bilaterally or in groups. Much of the work is also undertaken in the administrative space where discussions are held without any formal positions to explore and examine specific issues and wider considerations.

[38] Morphet, J. (2013) *How Europe shapes British public policy*, Bristol: Policy Press.

The EU also works within specific time frames of seven-year programmes[39] and budgets to allow each member state to have a general election during the period and if necessary have a formal policy reset. In the UK, this is done through processes known as the machinery of government that occur when there is a general election or a cabinet reshuffle or when functions are transferred between departments. In order to promote policy development and delivery, the EU has also positively encouraged relationships across all member states through common issue groups – smart cities, mayors or through neighbouring areas in macro[40] regions such as the Baltic or the Adriatic or across borders[41] as in the island of Ireland, around Luxembourg and across the Polish, Czech and German borders.

Within the EU, the political culture of the member states has also been absorbed. In many member states, governments are frequently coalitions and have pragmatic ways of working.[42] Many of the member states have experienced movements of people and changing political boundaries. This has created in many a desire for political stability. In some parts of the EU, these borders are with third countries such as Russia and Turkey.

Since its inception, the EU has been growing rather than decreasing. The possibility of a country leaving has never been a real consideration. When Greece was on the brink of its economic crisis, everything was done by other member states to keep the country within the EU. For this reason, the proposal to hold a referendum in the UK that might result in the UK leaving the EU was never fully considered. Just as the

[39] Goetz, Klaus H. and Meyer-Sahling, Jan-Hinrik (eds) (2012) *The EU Timescape*, London: Routledge.

[40] European Commission, 'Macro-Regional Strategies', http://ec.europa.eu/ regional_policy/en/policy/cooperation/macro-regional-strategies/

[41] European Commission, 'Interreg A – Cross-border cooperation', http:// ec.europa.eu/regional_policy/en/policy/cooperation/european-territorial/ cross-border/

[42] Mount, Ferdinand (2016) 'Nigels against the World', *London Review of Books*, 19 May, vol 38, no 12, pp 21–3, www.lrb.co.uk/v38/n10/ferdinand-mount/nigels-against-the-world

UK government and civil service was ill-prepared for this outcome, so were the EU institutions. This coloured their final offer to the UK government prior to the referendum in February 2016, which they located within the UK's past dealing with the EU and its demands as an anathema to the fundamental principles of the single market – the free movement of goods, services, capital and people. They were adopting a position based on a unified position between the other 27 members and saw no reason to shift their position.

When the result of the referendum was known, the EU was in shock with some senior politicians in tears. What the EU could not anticipate was that the UK referendum result was not going to be a unique event where a popularist vote gave a mandate for disruptive change over the established political order. The election of Trump as US president has provided further pause for thought inside the EU, not least when there are further threats to its longer term existence following general elections in France, Germany and the Netherlands in 2017, together with a rerun of the vote for the Austrian President, where a right wing candidate was defeated and the constitutional referendum in Italy where the Prime Minister was defeated and resigned. There are five opportunities for the population of Europe to express a view on the future role and direction of the EU by December 2017. Any or all of these could have a significant effect on its future.

All of this will mean that the EU has to reconsider its operational modes and to express more explicitly what it does for member states. It has a reputation that it is associated with economic liberalism and globalisation in countries that favour a more welfarist state system that has been predominant since 1945. The global migrant crisis has brought tensions within small communities unfamiliar with outsiders. Finally, Trump, with his America First rhetoric, may no longer be willing for the US to act as the world's policeman. Trump wants to make deals with former enemies including Russia in order to gain trading advantages brought through a more stable political situation. Trump has already indicated that NATO members must start to pay their own way and not be dependent on the US. He sees the way forward as reforming treaties on the EU's borders by making more wide ranging agreements rather than through threatening acts. This means that the EU cannot rely on this protection on defence and security matters from the US and this will be compounded following Brexit.

Therefore, the EU is facing a future where it needs to examine its own operating assumptions. It has conceptualised its role as being progressive and redistributive, and brings better standards of living achieved through political stability and increased market scale as its size has grown. It has assumed that the charges of political distance and unaccountability have been answered through increasing powers for the directly elected Parliament. This process will encourage the EU to assess and consider the benefits that it has brought to all its member states and Europe as a whole. It will also need to consider how it defends its role from both internal attack and external threats. It needs to reconceptualise and communicate its role to generations that have no experience of war. It has to consider how to relocate itself in a world without the UK as a member and understand what this future relationship will be. It will also need to consider whether the sanctity of the four single market freedoms, particularly free movement of people, undermines its wider purposes and stability. Nevertheless, the EU can make this consideration on the basis of its wealth of experience of cooperation and the gains that it has made over its history that are discussed next.

Being inside the largest world market

The EU is now the largest market in the world and the UK does most of its trade within this market. The free movement of goods within the EU is based on the removal of customs and tariffs through the use of common regulations for goods and services across the single market area.[43] The country that the UK trades with the most is the US, although this may change following Trump's new economic

---

[43] European Parliament (2016) 'Free Movement of Goods', Fact Sheets on the European Union, www.europarl.europa.eu/RegData/etudes/fiches_techniques/2013/030102/04A_FT(2013)030102_EN.pdf

protectionist orthodoxy and deal making. Within the EU, trade is undertaken through the single market where rules and standards are being harmonised, where professional qualifications are accepted across member states and where goods can be made and sold with ease without the need for customs points and cross border bureaucracy. There is also free movement of services and capital for investment that allows the trade between countries to operate under different regulatory regimes. There are further areas of the single market to be developed but overall European economies and consumers have benefited from an increase in cross border rights, including common regulations for goods and services. The single market has also promoted initiatives to help small and medium sized enterprises within different sectors of the economy.[44]

Externally, the EU negotiates on behalf of all member states with the World Trade Organization and is also responsible for member states' compliance on treaties concerning goods and services and access to public sector markets. Through these negotiations, the European Commission can trade off member state requirements and use their larger negotiating power to achieve ends that might not be possible for individual states. The EU has also negotiated some specific trade arrangements with the WTO such as that for agriculture that allows extra payments to be made to farmers and in rural areas. The EU has also negotiated 52 other trade agreements,[45] including the latest with Canada in 2016. These trade agreements are primarily focused on goods rather than services although these were included in the proposed Transatlantic Trade and Investment Partnership (TTIP) deal with the US.

In the sphere of financial services, the single market operates for some financial transfers for banks and financial bodies recognised as operating

---

[44] European Parliament (2016), 'Challenges and opportunities for Europe's small transport firms, At a glance', Plenary – 18 November, www.europarl. europa.eu/RegData/etudes/ATAG/2016/593533/EPRS_ATA(2016)593533_ EN.pdf

[45] European Commission, 'Trade – Policy – Countries and regions', http:// ec.europa.eu/trade/policy/countries-and-regions

within this sector. Within the EU, London is the largest trading centre for financial services in Europe, US and eastern markets. It houses many European headquarters of banks and insurance companies and is also the centre of hedge funds and secondary markets. The financial services sector also has associated expertise in legal and accounting services. The EU is bringing forward greater regulation to financial services and working on issues such as tax offshoring, where businesses can move their tax liabilities away from the country where profits are made to others where payment rates are less. The movement of finance within the EU is achieved by processes known as 'passporting', which operate in much the same way as the movement of people. The UK has been a leading member state in the development of these approaches and, prior to the referendum, the UK's EU Commissioner was responsible for financial stability, financial services and the capital markets union.

The continuation of these systems, including passporting, will need to be specifically negotiated by the UK as part of any Brexit deal. Further, London is potentially less appealing to non-EU banks and institutions that require a location inside the single market. Meanwhile, banks and financial institutions are taking offices or expanding their teams inside other member states as the financial regulators are asking them to act to minimise and mitigate any potential risks for their investors following Brexit. Some companies have already stated that they will be moving their headquarters outside the UK.

In the past, other businesses from outside the EU have located within the UK as a gateway to EU markets and this was a policy particularly promoted by Thatcher. These include Japanese car companies such as Nissan and Toyota and US insurance companies and banks. The Prime Minister has stated that her intention is that the UK leaves the Single Market and the customs union but that she would then seek selective deals for specific sectors.

The EU is also concerned with how markets are functioning when there is competition from third countries. One example of this is the growth in competition in aviation and the EC has sought permission from the member states to start negotiations on trade agreements with a range of other countries including China, ASEAN, Mexico and Kuwait.[46]

Being part of a global diplomatic group

The EU has had a growing diplomatic service across the world since it appointed a High Representative for foreign affairs in 2007. Since then, the EU has been able to increasingly offer a single coordinated voice in negotiation and has been recognised as a significant contributor to a number of peace agreements including that in Iran. The EU increasingly coordinates member states diplomats abroad and provides opportunities to discuss and use common positions to its advantage.[47] This is likely to continue in the future and may no longer be available to the UK following Brexit.

The pressures on the EU since the economic crisis in 2008 have meant that it has to think further about developing its external foreign policies and to integrate them more into its regular considerations of issues rather than responding to them as specific events. For this reason, it has been reviewing its foreign policies alongside its defence and security policies. The pressures on the EU both politically and diplomatically following the refugee crisis have also meant that it needs to consider its position, not least as its relationship with Turkey, as an aspirant member state, has worsened since the internal unrest during 2016. The President of Turkey has now threatened to release the refugee migrants currently in Turkey into the EU if it does not continue to engage with Turkey's candidacy for EU membership. This

---

[46] European Parliament (2016) 'International aviation agreements, At a glance', Plenary – 18 November, www.europarl.europa.eu/RegData/etudes/ATAG/2016/593524/EPRS_ATA(2016)593524_EN.pdf

[47] Centre for European Reform (2016) 'Brexit and foreign policy: divorce?', Bulletin article, 18 July, www.cer.org.uk/publications/archive/bulletin-article/2016/brexit-and-foreign-policy-divorce; Whitman, R.G. (2016) 'Brexit or Bremain: what future for the UK's European diplomatic strategy?', *International Affairs*, vol 91, no 3, pp 509–29, http://ukandeu.ac.uk/wp-content/uploads/2016/05/International-Affairs-Brexit-or-Bremain.pdf

kind of pressure and deal making is most similar to the new Trump methods of undertaking deal-making foreign policy and more of this approach may follow.

The other issue to consider is that, post Brexit, the UK will have to increase its range of diplomatic effort and networking with EU member states to bring about what influence it can from outside. UK diplomats will no longer meet colleagues from other countries at regular meetings and have an inside position on negotiations and support for its interests that is currently provided through the burgeoning foreign service. This ability to engage through these means was assessed as an asset in the Foreign and Commonwealth Office's balance of competences review in 2014.

Defence and security

The UK works with the EU on defence and security. In November 2016, the European Parliament voted to implement common foreign and security policy. The MEPs called for more unity and a robust foreign and security policy to be established. The Treaty of Lisbon provided for the EU to take full responsibility of its own security through Permanent Structured Cooperation (PESCO), which allows for some member states to cooperate closely in defence and for others to join later if they wish. The EU's diplomatic external action service will be strengthened by these decisions.

As a result of the Trump election in the US, the EU is likely to press towards defence and security cooperation more rapidly, including the potential for establishing a common army. The UK has benefited from the current security and defence policy approach as it has been able to contribute and lead this and has access to information and intelligence. There is an increased role on defence and security cooperation being played by NATO including on cyber security. Further, France, Germany and the UK have defence policies that are converging with an intention that the EU and NATO, both Brussels based institutions, will work more closely together.

Despite the Prime Minister's commitment to maintaining and strengthening EU ties on defence and security, made in her Lancaster House speech,[48] the expectation is that Brexit will damage this cooperation within the EU as it will remove the layer of political collaboration that supports dialogue.[49] The development of the common defence and security policy has been effective and efficient for the UK.[50] It provides a larger voice for the UK and it has provided a means of influence into the policies of the other member states and the EU. It has also enabled the development of common positions prior to engaging in wider international debate, for example over the sanctions imposed on Russia after the incursions into the Crimea. Trying to exert a similar amount of influence from outside the EU will not only take time but the other member states will have developed common positions without the UK and these may be less open to influence and oppositional to a UK preferred position. The UK may be able to negotiate a specific status post Brexit in this policy area such as an associated member but this is by no means guaranteed.

Benefiting from environmental standards

Since 1972, the EU has had a strong focus and commitment to achieving higher environmental standards across the EU. This is because the environment and its associated issues are defined as being borderless with the effects from one country easily transferred to another whether this is water quality or other polluting activity. Some

[48] www.gov.uk/government/speeches/the-governments-negotiating-objectives-for-exiting-the-eu-pm-speech

[49] House of Commons Library (2016) 'Defence and security after Brexit: a reading list', 19 October, http://researchbriefings.parliament.uk/ResearchBriefing/Summary/CBP-7742

[50] Whitman, R.G. (2016) 'The UK and EU foreign, security and defence policy after Brexit: integrated, associated or detached?', *National Institute Economic Review*, no 238, November, http://ukandeu.ac.uk/wp-content/uploads/2016/11/The-UK-and-EU-foreign-security-and-defense-policy-after-Brexit.pdf

countries may attempt to offset their obligations through dumping their waste or toxic materials in other countries. The EU has always adopted a polluter pays principle and this has been upheld in practice.

The EU has promoted its environmental priorities in a number of ways including being a full and active participant and deliverer of the UN's environmental, sustainability and climate change initiatives. The EU has included environmental standards and outcomes within the single market as a core policy. The EU also monitors compliance, taking cases of member state non-delivery to the European Court of Justice. The EU negotiated for all member states in the UN's Paris Accord on climate change, fast-tracked its ratification so that it had sufficient signatories and could be brought into force. Each member state still has to confirm its agreement individually and the UK has completed this, although after France and Germany.[51]

The EU is now working on implementing the United Nations' Sustainable Development Goals, including for example Goal 16 (peace, justice, rule of law, inclusive and accountable institutions).[52] In promoting these goals, the EU brings together all of the EU institutions to work together in considering how they can be implemented and delivered. The EU also has a common position on issues such as the Arctic[53] where it is willing and able to use its structural and investment funds to support economic development and jobs there. This strategy also recognises both the strategic role of the Arctic and also the need to tackle climate change issues and to promote international cooperation.

While the UK has a reasonable environmental record, much of this has been brought about through this EU context. When the environmental agenda was first fully developed in the mid-1980s,

---

[51] 'Paris Agreement and Marrakech Climate Conference', 25 November 2016, http://researchbriefings.parliament.uk/ResearchBriefing/Summary/CBP-7718

[52] United Nations, 'Sustainable development goals', www.un.org/sustainabledevelopment/sustainable-development-goals

[53] European Parliament Think Tank (2016) 'EU regional policy in the Arctic, 21 November, www.europarl.europa.eu/thinktank/en/document.html?reference=EPRS_BRI(2016)593530

the UK government did not take this seriously and assumed that the environmental standards were aspirational rather than firm targets for matters such as air quality, waste, water and habitats. The UK has learned to its cost, through fines paid into the European Court of Justice, that its non-compliance on the directives for air quality and environmental impact for example will not be tolerated or overlooked.

The relationship between the UK and the EU after Brexit on environmental issues and regulations will depend on the final agreements reached. The UN has called for the UK to stay linked to the EU on these policies on the basis that cross border issues will persist.[54] For organisations and companies operating within the single market, then the environmental obligations will remain. Outside the single market, free trade area or customs union, the UK will need to negotiate new relationships with others. In the short term the UK is likely to transpose EU legislation into UK domestic law but, over time, as the EU is strengthening its approach and delivery of environmental objectives, there may be pressure on the UK to liberalise and to reduce the standards that it adopts with the environment being left in a more vulnerable position.[55]

Having a focus on equity

The EU has social, economic and territorial cohesion as its core principles and through its cohesion programme among others it takes active steps to reduce disparities within and across its area. One of the instruments it uses is the European Regional Development Fund (ERDF) which operates through investment and cooperation

---

[54] Neslen, A. (2016) 'UN calls for post-Brexit UK to link with EU on environment policy', *Guardian*, 6 July, www.theguardian.com/environment/2016/jul/06/un-calls-for-post-brexit-uk-to-link-with-eu-on-environment-policy

[55] Institute for European Environmental Policy (2016) *The potential policy and environmental consequences for the UK of a departure from the European Union*, March, www.ieep.eu/assets/2000/IEEP_Brexit_2016.pdf

programmes.[56] The issue of equity is being tackled through other specific measures, such as the work of the European Bank for Reconstruction and Development, although there is recognition that market liberalisation and globalisation has not helped equality as much as first envisaged.[57]

These cohesion principles have affected EU policy in a number of ways that include consideration of the effects of peripherality and islands, low skills, low income and youth unemployment. Specific policies are designed to address these issues and are accompanied by spending programmes and projects to focus on improving the lives of those in this position.

There are also strong policies for equality issues in the workplace and access to services that are reinforced through legislation and programme delivery. Since the UK referendum there have been concerns that Brexit will lead to a diminution of these standards and lower worker protection rights than exist at present. These rights are aligned to those available through human rights legislation that will remain as they are outside the EU but the EU equality measures are the first line of defence for most people. Since the referendum there have also been an increase in hate crimes and the UK's Equality and Human Rights Commission wrote to all political parties in late November 2016 asking them to tone down their rhetoric and to respect those on both sides of the argument.

Being networked into our geographical neighbours

One of the major strengths of the EU is the emphasis that it places on cross border and cross national working between sub-state local and regional bodies. Through series of projects that have been operating

---

[56] European Parliament (2016) 'European Regional Development Fund (ERDF)', Fact Sheets on the European Union, www.europarl.europa.eu/RegData/etudes/fiches_techniques/2013/050102/04A_FT(2013)050102_EN.pdf

[57] European Bank for Reconstruction and Development (EBRD) (2016) *Transition Report 2016–17*, http://2016.tr-ebrd.com

since 1992, the Interreg programme,[58] cross border projects that have encompassed both physical infrastructure improvements to enable people to cross borders for work and social and cultural projects to encourage better relationships and to attract visitors have been important.

As part of this process the EU has also started to encourage parts of the EU to work together on economic and environmental plans. These started in 1994 and have since developed into macroeconomic strategies[59] that have been adopted by all the EU institutions which have approved their support for their delivery. These macro regional plans and programmes now exist for the Baltic Sea, the Adriatic, the Danube and the Alps regions. The plans consider how the necessary economic and environmental programmes within the macro region can be developed and implemented through joint working.

Following Brexit, the UK will not have access to these programmes unless through specific negotiation or through another member state. Cross border working is a particular issue on the island of Ireland and at present it is difficult to see what future means of working can be adopted.[60] There may be some possibilities through the British–Irish Council,[61] which could allow some joint and cross border working through Ireland particularly using an EU legal construct such as a European Grouping of Territorial Cooperation.[62] At present the UK is not part of a macro region although it is hard to see what effect this might have when these macro regional strategies with their associated plans and programmes move further west across Europe.

[58] European Commission, 'Interreg A – Cross-border cooperation'.
[59] European Commission, 'Macro-Regional Strategies'.
[60] Centre for Cross Border Studies, http://crossborder.ie/
[61] British-Irish Council, www.britishirishcouncil.org
[62] European Grouping of Territorial Cooperation (EGTC), https://portal.cor.europa.eu/egtc/Pages/welcome.aspx

Having energy security

The development of the Energy Union is a major priority for the EU at present. This focuses on security of supply, the reduction of carbon, increased renewable energy supply and the promotion of reductions in energy consumption. It is also concerned with energy pricing and market competition across and within energy sectors. The EU has also set renewable targets across the EU and each member state is meeting these through their own preferred methods.

The UK Foreign Office EU Balance of Competences Review in 2014 showed that the UK had benefited considerably from EU energy policy. Although the UK had provision of energy through North Sea oil and gas, this supply is reducing and the UK is now more reliant on external sources particularly through EU member states. The UK imports half of its gas and two-thirds of this is transported through pipelines connecting to EU countries and about 6.5% of UK electricity consumption is imported. The EU is supporting the delivery of more physical interconnectors to improve both the supply of energy and to enable UK consumers to take advantage of lower energy prices.

On leaving the EU, post Brexit, UK energy supplies are expected to be adequate in the short term. In the medium to long term, supplies of gas are considered to be adequate. However, supplies of electricity may no longer benefit from EU wholesale prices and have supply capacity issues.[63] The UK could overcome this by investing in low fuel technologies and retrofitting buildings – both domestic and commercial/industrial – but this will take time. It could also invest in more wind power and other renewables to make up the deficit, although some of these sources will need pipeline investment to take them from the coast to connect with the National Grid.[64] The UK

---

[63] UCL Institute for Sustainable Resources (2016) 'Brexit and Energy: Cost, Security and Climate Policy Implications', 25 May, www.bartlett.ucl.ac.uk/sustainable/sustainable-news/brexit-and-energy

[64] Halfpenny-Ray, S. (2016) 'Brexit Briefing: Energy Security', Canterbury Christ Church University, www.canterbury.ac.uk/social-and-applied-sciences/

may be able to join the Energy Community or have an agreement such as that between the EU and Norway for energy but this would need to be negotiated and agreed. Chatham House, the foreign policy think tank, has argued that leaving the EU's energy relationships is not an option for the UK as it would diminish the UK's influence on energy policy both within the EU and outside it within international relations[65] as well as potentially endangering supply.

Having a common macroprudential framework

The economic crisis in 2007 led the EU to examine its position in relation to its own macroprudential policies for the single market and for the member states' economies. Through a review of the single market undertaken by the former Italian Prime Minister Monti, the EU reset its economic goals and agreed that it would consider the reduction in regulations to free up the market but also to address areas where less progress had been made. This review and its recommendations were included within Europe 2020,[66] a new macroeconomic plan for the EU which not only focused on what the EU should be doing centrally but the ways in which each member state should be addressing their economic weaknesses to contribute to the whole. The EC identified the economic weaknesses in member states, discussed how they might be addressed and since 2012[67] has undertaken six monthly reviews

psychology-politics-and-sociology/cefeus/docs/brexit-briefing-energy-security.pdf

[65] Chatham House (2016) 'UK Unplugged? The Impacts of Brexit on Energy and Climate Policy', Research Paper, May, www.chathamhouse.org/sites/files/chathamhouse/publications/research/2016-05-26-uk-unplugged-brexit-energy-froggatt-raines-tomlinson.pdf

[66] European Parliament (2016) 'Role of the European Council in delivery of single market strategies', Briefing, European Council in Action, November, www.europarl.europa.eu/RegData/etudes/BRIE/2016/593784/EPRS_BRI(2016)593784_EN.pdf

[67] European Parliament (2016) 'Briefing: The EU macro-prudential policy framework', PE 587.379, 22 November, www.europarl.europa.eu/RegData/etudes/BRIE/2016/587379/IPOL_BRI(2016)587379_EN.pdf

of progress towards improving performance. The delivery of these goals was also included within all the subsequent programmes for the seven-year cycle 2014–20 and in cohesion programmes.

The EC identified the UK economic weaknesses as being planning, infrastructure, housing and youth skills and since the beginning of this programme, the government has been active in numerous ways in an attempt to improve its performance in these four areas. Initially the Treasury regarded planning as the key to improving performance in housing and infrastructure but has subsequently found that even where planning systems have been improved, the problems in delivering housing and infrastructure depend on the private sector implementing these consents.[68]

A second area of policy that has emerged as part of the Europe 2020 programme within the UK has been the Citydeals that are vertical contracts between localities, national governments where they exist, central government and the EU. These focus on specific outcomes informed by the UK's overall macroprudential weaknesses and have been implemented all over the UK including in Belfast, Wales and the whole of Scotland.

What does the UK do for the EU?

The UK contributes to the EU in a number of ways. First, it offers experience and access through its role on the UN Security Council and as a member of the G7 and G20. Second, the UK holds considerable soft power within the world and is able to draw people together to discuss international issues such as the actions of Prime Minister Gordon Brown during the global economic crisis in 2007–08. The UK has also had traditionally good relationships with the US although these are now shifting with more direct discussions on the EU taking place through Germany.

Until the Brexit referendum, the UK was the world's fifth largest market, which made the EU the largest market in the world; without

[68] www.gov.uk/government/collections/housing-white-paper

the UK, the EU market will be smaller than the US. The UK is respected on defence and security policy and has a reputation of engaging with global conflicts. The UK also commits to international aid through its GDP percentage commitment. The UK has a reputation of being a fair dealer and being a stable country that has attracted investment and business. The UK is also known as being an open economy and this has sometimes been an advantage within the EU in supporting more free trade. The UK is also a centre for culture and the use of English across the international community and the Commonwealth has meant that it has considerable influence.

All of these contributions and others will be lost to the EU when the UK leaves. The EU will change its formation and consider how its priorities will be managed without the UK. The election of Trump to the US presidency may suggest that the EU will value the UK's continued presence more than before the referendum and this may change and influence its negotiating position with the UK.

THREE

What are the options for future UK/EU institutional relationships?

Introduction

Much of the discussion on the form of Brexit since the referendum has been about whether this will be a hard Brexit or a soft Brexit. These terms are also as much polarised as the leave and remain campaign positions and many of those who would rather remain are campaigning for a soft Brexit if one has to be achieved at all. There was very little discussion of the form of Brexit that might follow a leave vote before the referendum, although those campaigning for leave have linked a hard Brexit narrative to the leave campaign arguing that this is what people voted for.

The options for Brexit agreements are many and various and in this chapter some of the main forms that Brexit could take are outlined and discussed. The choice of option or negotiated outcome of triggering Article 50 could be based on one of these. However, it is important to consider what the UK is seeking to obtain from these negotiations as being in its own best interest and as yet this has not been stated by the government[1] although it may emerge in parliamentary debates. In practice, none of these negotiating positions or 'asks' may be their final form. However, in any agreement there are a number of key elements that shape the differences between Brexit models. Understanding the provenance and associated implications for the many potential forms of Brexit may assist in evaluating the options when there is discussion about the proposed final agreement and provide some frameworks for assessing the likely longer-term implications for the UK beyond Brexit.

The models that are under consideration here also reflect the more complex relationship that the UK has with the EU than is generally understood. These are discussed in more detail in Chapter Two but broadly divide into those relationships where the EU acts as a negotiator for agreements and assures subsequent compliance of its members to international bodies including the World Trade Organization (WTO) on trade and the United Nations (UN) on environment and some maritime issues. The European Commission (EC) has direct powers over issues such as the internal single market and macroeconomic policy and, on the latter, develops and applies policy based on advice from other international bodies such as the International Monetary Fund (IMF) and the Organization for Economic Cooperation and Development (OECD).

In terms of decision making for policy development and delivery within the EU, the UK takes decisions on issues such as international aid, foreign policy, some fiscal priorities and how EU legislation should be delivered. This EU legislation is agreed by all member states through a range of decision processes within the EU including the Council of Ministers and other mechanisms such as COREPER (Committee of Permanent Representatives), a committee of officials than can progress legislation if there are no member state objections. In some areas of legislation, member states operating through the Council of Ministers share their responsibilities with the European Parliament and, in others, member state vetoes may operate. Thus for

[1]   BBC News (2016) 'Downing Street dismisses Brexit 'divisions' memo', 15 November, www.bbc.co.uk/news/uk-politics-37983948

any agreement on negotiations on the future relationships between the EU and the UK, generated through invoking Article 50, there will have to be agreement between the member states based on the prevailing decision model for that specific piece of legislation. The agreement model for any Article 50 package will need to observe these principles. In some options, it would be possible for all member states other than the UK to agree an approach and that would be binding on the UK as part of an agreement.

The negotiations on Article 50 and subsequent EU–UK relations are being led by representatives of the President of the Council, by the European Parliament and by the EC. All three are experienced politicians and negotiators in their own countries and within the EU. They are likely to operate informally as a group but on occasion may adopt different positions that reflect priorities of the part of the EU that they are representing or in order to achieve a decision combining soft and hard negotiation techniques between them. The rhetoric and tone of the negotiations varies from day to day and relates to the position of the individual making the statement. In France, with general elections in 2017, there is a focus on being tough with the UK in order to discourage a similar move for a referendum from the far right. Similarly, in Germany, the rhetoric is tough although more nuanced, as the general elections also fall at the end of 2017. The Polish Prime Minister has said that she will be helpful and supportive of Brexit if the UK considers its positions and is more flexible. In other member states the tone of Brexit comments depends on the issue and wider external pressures.

In the United States, the Obama administration was against Brexit and it is likely that there was strong US pressure behind the scenes for the EU and the UK to shift their positions. President Trump has taken a stance on protectionism within the US as his favoured trade model and prefers bilateral agreements rather than large trade groups. He has supported Brexit although drawing up a practical and implementable trade deal with the UK, may take some time, whether there is a special relationship or not. The IMF is concerned about the effects of Brexit on the longer-term global economic position. The extent to which any trade agreement with other countries is worth pursuing depends on the view about the amount of international trade any country needs for a successful economy. The UK has always been a trading nation. However, both the rise of popularism against globalisation of trade and the rise of economic theories that approximately 50% of trade in any country is undertaken between domestic markets[2] may mean some rethinking on the longer-term trade model for the UK. In effect, the question is whether the UK will find other countries with the appetite for trading relationships and what will its position be once outside the EU's single market, if that occurs. Will it become dependent on the provision of goods and services domestically and will this be enough?

The EU's negotiating positions are not clear. From the EU, it is important to consider the overall commitment to the political basis of the European Union in many member states. For the founding members, there remains a wish to avoid the kind of conflict last experienced in the two world wars in the 20th century. For the Eastern European member states, the so called Visegrad group, there is a wish to escape the former dominance of Russia although it is clear that in some of these countries there is a desire to return to the kind of certainties that the communist regime offered. This group has already stated that it could veto a Brexit deal.[3] For the island states, Malta, Cyprus and Ireland, there is a concern to be at the table and not in an isolated periphery. They are also all likely to develop a more independent line away from the UK and towards the EU.[4] The same

[2] Krugman, P. (1991) *Geography and Trade*, Cambridge, MA: MIT Press; Krugman, P. (2011) 'The new economic geography, now middle-aged', *Regional Studies*, vol 45, no 1, pp 1–8.
[3] BBC News (2016) 'Visegrad Group of EU states "could veto Brexit deal"', 17 September, www.bbc.co.uk/news/world-europe-37396805
[4] Pace, R. (2015) 'Should Brexit materialise, UK influence in Malta is likely to diminish', The UK in a Changing Europe, 30 September, http://ukandeu.ac.uk/should-brexit-materialise-uk-influence-in-malta-is-likely-to-diminish; SigmaLive (2016) 'Moody's: Brexit to have increased impact in Cyprus', 12 July, www.sigmalive.com/en/news/economy/146907/moodys-brexit-to-have-increased-impact-in-cyprus; The Economist (2016) 'Ireland

applies to Scandinavian states that also prefer to be part of a larger group with its increased access to power and a defence against former enemies – Russia and Germany. The Club Med also recognises that the power of the north of Europe together with its purchasing power is essential for their longer-term economic interests. There are also many other economic, social and political drivers for the member states to be EU members.

However, it is likely that the wider concerns that are more important than specific economic interests will form an important basis for decision making within EU member states. Jonathan Hill, UK EU Commissioner until the referendum, has argued that there are two important issues for the UK to understand in the negotiating process. The first is that those who are strongly in support of the EU as an economic and political project, including the EC and member states, find it hard to consider that Brexit will ever occur in practice. They are working on the assumption that the economic effects of Brexit on the UK together with wider international pressure from the US and global financial institutions will mean that the UK will reconsider its position. They also assume that this will be achieved through a way that is found within the UK. This may be through MPs voting down Article 50 – at either end of its process (to trigger it or to accept the proposals negotiated through it) or that there will be another referendum – an approach that has been used in other member states including France, Ireland and Denmark. Another approach will be the legal challenge to determine whether the UK leaves the European Economic Area at the same time as it leaves the EU. If this judicial review finds that this requires a separate process or did not form part of the referendum decision, the UK could remain part of the single market.

In attempting to affirm the decision to leave through the UK referendum to his former EU colleagues, Hill also has a message for those undertaking the negotiations in the UK. He argues that the

may suffer the most from Brexit', 29 October, www.economist.com/news/europe/21709354-making-it-one-few-european-countries-wants-be-kind-britain-ireland-may-suffer extent of the emotional ties of member states to the European Union is so great that they are quite likely to offer an arrangement to the UK that may be against their economic interests if the UK can be persuaded to remain within the EU. As yet it is uncertain what this might mean but examples of manoeuvrability are likely to emerge in 2018 after the French and German general elections.

The pressures on agreeing a Brexit model are primarily time constrained. These constraints are determined by the next UK general election in May 2020 and the new EU budgetary and programme period that is linked with changes in Commissioners and those in lead positions that will occur in 2020 prior to the new programme period 2021–27. The UK has also ready foregone its period as Chair of the European Council in 2017 and this, together with the two-year period following the triggering of Article 50, determined the optimum date for calling the UK referendum. This meant that the UK did not have to spend six months promoting new initiatives in the EU but it was also a major opportunity foregone to introduce legislation and negotiated initiatives that may have changed the nature of the Brexit debate within the UK.

Why do these models matter?

The models of future UK/EU arrangements that are set out below and are summarised in Table 3.1 provide a means of identifying the implications of each one for the UK. This table does not suggest a weighting or ranking between these options – that will be for the reader to determine based on their own priorities for the future of the UK and/or the EU. However, they can provide a framework for examining the options. Frequently when these models are discussed individually, there is an emphasis on specific or unique features that determine the model without considering other implications. Further, in anticipation of the known unknowns, it is important to review the potential unintended consequences of each model including those opportunities that have been missed. There is also a need to bear in mind unknown unknowns that might be related to wider geopolitical turmoil or change, the implications of environmental disaster or other events that cannot be anticipated at the moment. There may also be cumulative consequences of these individual models that emerge as they are discussed further or applied in practice. Perhaps the main issue to be aware of is that it is unlikely that any single model will remain stable. The relationship between the EU and the UK will have features of many of these models and over time they will interrelate, change and mutate.

Table 3.1: A summary of the content of alternative options for the UK

Policy/ legislative area	Current	Norway model	Switzerland model	Canada	Free trade model	Greenland option	
						in	out
Regulations and directives							
Free movement							
Customs union							
Payment							
rebate							
Informal agreements							
Infrastructure programmes: TEN-T – legislation and funding							
TEN-E (energy) – legislation and funding							
Cohesion programmes, incl. transport, regen, rural, ports, R&D, skills (frequently put in LEP growth deals)							

Policy/ legislative area	Current	Norway model	Switzerland model	Canada	Free trade model	Greenland option	
						in	out
Cohesion funding							
Access to EIB finance							
ESDP mark 2							
Urban Pact planning regulations							
Single market			selective		selective		
Competition (WTO)							
Agricultural mkt regulation (WTO)							
Combined authorities (OECD)							
Pressure on planning reform, housing and infrastructure (IMF; OECD)							
Environment/ climate change (UN)							

What models are there?

Same but different: the bespoke model

This is the Prime Minister's preferred option as stated in her Lancaster House speech in January 2017. Although many commentators regard the potential of a new offer from the EU to the UK as wishful thinking on the part of remainers, it is a very likely part of the process of negotiation. The external pressure on the EU to find a way to make a new deal or relationship with the UK is very strong and the

UK's Foreign Minister has hinted at it following major meetings at international events outside the EU such as those in the UN.

What might a revised offer include? First, the many different relationships that the EU has with both member and non-member states offer more flexibility than the headlines might suggest. There are some countries such as Liechtenstein that appear to have controlled labour movement for example in their agreement with the EU and a discussion based on this principle might be considered to be enough for the government to reverse its position. Second, the kind of relationships that the UK wants such as those on trade for cars may only be offered on the basis of some other requirements. The UK may by this time be so wedded to these special deals that they will seek some kind of remain status. Third, the EU might require that the UK has another referendum as part of its own Article 50 negotiations.

These options may sound impossible but the effect of one of these revised offers being accepted would be that, apart from that specific set of points in a new agreement, then all the other parts of the UK's membership of the EU would remain the same.

The European Economic Area: the Norway model

The European Economic Area (EEA)[5] was founded in 1994 and comprises all members of the EU and is open to all members of the European Free Trade Association (EFTA), which includes all EU member states, Iceland, Norway and Liechtenstein and Switzerland. All of these countries, with the exception of Switzerland, belong to the EEA that provides for free movement of people, goods, services and capital between its members and those members of the Single European Market. EEA members accept all EU legislation in relation to the single market with the exception of that on agriculture and fisheries.

[5] European Parliament (2016) 'The European Economic Area (EEA), Switzerland and the North', Fact Sheets on the European Union, www.europarl.europa.eu/RegData/etudes/fiches_techniques/2013/060503/04A_FT(2013)060503_EN.pdf

There is some dispute as to whether if the UK triggers Article 50 to leave the EU it will at the same time trigger a process to leave the EEA. Those in favour of Brexit argue that they are the same thing but a cross-party group in favour of remaining in the single market took this decision to judicial review to determine whether it is lawful to trigger Article 127 of the EEA agreement to leave this at the same time but were not successful.

EEA members are not members of the EU although they have to accept all the single market legislation without being able to vote on it with the EU member states, although EEA members are able to contribute to the discussions on legislation before it is adopted.[6] Norway, like other EEA members, also has to ensure that all of its domestic law is compliant with the terms of its membership. The EEA countries also make payments to the EU and have an annual grant from the EU to reduce social and economic disparities (or cohesion).

The EEA is outside the EU's VAT agreement and EEA members set their own VAT rates. The EEA does not cover other areas of EU membership including freedom, security and justice although it does include membership of discussions and agreement on issues such as counter-terrorism. Norway is not part of the customs union and so undertakes customs checks between Norway and EU member states and does not give access to trade deals agreed by the EU with third countries. However, Norway is part of the Schengen area for free movement.

In the EEA or Norway model, the UK would have access to the single market apart from agriculture and fisheries unless this is specifically negotiated. This EEA membership would be in return for payment of a similar fee to that paid now and the adoption of

[6]   HM Government (2016) 'Alternatives to membership: possible models for the United Kingdom outside the European Union', www.gov.uk/government/uploads/system/uploads/attachment_data/file/504604/Alternatives_to_membership_-_possible_models_for_the_UK_outside_the_EU.pdf

the four freedoms for capital, goods, services and labour. The UK would receive no rebate and no funding for infrastructure projects and may receive some funding to promote cohesion in common with other EEA members. Other regulatory requirements through the WTO such as for agriculture and trade remain.

The Norway model has been suggested as one of the options for the UK post Brexit. While being part of the single market, the UK would be outside agriculture and fisheries agreements and would also be free to negotiate its own agreements with other countries. This model is described as 'membership without a vote'.[7] It provides a means by which the UK could be independent and outside the political structures of the EU although it would also pay for its membership of the single market and customs union. It would also include a requirement for free movement of people, which may not be considered to meet the views expressed in the UK's referendum outcome. The UK may also not be able to use this route to EU markets as once the UK leaves the EU it will also leave the EEA. This membership would need to be re-negotiated through membership of EFTA, which would have to be approved by all four EFTA members. It has been suggested that Norway may not agree to the UK rejoining the EEA so this option may not be available.[8]

EFTA: the Switzerland model

Switzerland is a member of EFTA but not part of the EEA. Through EFTA membership, the UK would be able to negotiate some bilateral agreements with the EU and have some access to the single market,

---

[7] Chu, B. (2016) 'Could the 'Norway model' work for Britain? Yes, but we wouldn't be taking back control', *Independent*, 10 July, www.independent. co.uk/voices/brexit-eu-referendum-norway-single-market-could-the-norway-model-work-for-britain-yes-but-we-wouldnt-a7129246.html

[8] Mortimer, C. (2016) 'Brexit: Norway could block the UK from rejoining the Economic Free Trade Area', *Independent*, 9 August, www.independent.co.uk/news/world/europe/brexit-norway-uk-eu-block-veto-economic-free-trade-area-freedom-of-movement-a7181546.html

also through agreements. In order to gain access to the single market, Switzerland has had to agree the free movement of citizens and although this has recently been contested by the Swiss it has been upheld by the EU as part of their agreement. Switzerland does not have access to EU agreements on financial services. Switzerland is not part of the customs union and has spot rather than mandatory checks on goods and services crossing the border although all need to have complete documentation and be able to demonstrate regulatory compliance or face fines.

Under this model, the UK would have no access to influence EU policies and proposed legislation and this would be less than that offered under the EEA Norway model where there are some institutional structures in place for discussion and potential influence. However, the UK would pay a lower financial contribution which would cover policies such as research and it is calculated that this approach would lead to a reduction in the UK's contribution of 59%.[9]

Over the period since Switzerland voted not to join the EEA in 1992, over 100 individual bilateral deals have been agreed with the EU which primarily cover trade in goods. There are fewer bilateral agreements on the trade for services and Swiss restrictions on some professional free movement. Switzerland has not concluded bilateral agreements on financial services and has no passporting arrangements so Swiss banks have had to establish subsidiaries within the EU/EEA area.[10]

In terms of domestic law, the Swiss are obliged to align their own law to EU law where there are agreements for those areas and failure to do so will lead to Switzerland being excluded from the terms of that specific legislation within the EU and block Switzerland from the single market. It is also obliged to follow rules of competiton, state aid and the environment. Switzerland is part of the Schengen agreement.

---

[9] Slaughter and May (2016) 'Brexit essentials: Alternatives to EU membership', www.slaughterandmay.com/media/2535258/brexit-essentials-alternatives-to-eu-membership.pdf

[10] HM Government (2016) *Alternatives to membership.*

The relationship between Switzerland and the EU was meant to be transitional as a pathway to membership although this has not occurred. The EU agreement with Switzerland appears unlikely to be pursued with any other state and therefore may not be available to the UK.

Customs union: the Turkey model

Turkey has some access to the EU's single or internal market through its membership of the customs union that gives tariff free trade and a 'level playing field' for business[11] that also includes free movement of people. This agreement with the EU is based both on an economic agreement and Turkey's candidacy for membership of the EU. Access to the single market relates to industrial goods and processed agricultural products where customs checks are not required but do not apply to raw agricultural products or services. In areas where Turkey has access to the EU market, it is required to enforce rules that are equivalent to those in the EU. This includes competition, product and environmental rules. Turkey is also required to align rules on state aid (government support to businesses) with EU rules. The agreement with Turkey provides some limited migration rights for Turkish nationals to reside in the EU. The EU also negotiates with the WTO on behalf of Turkey.[12]

Under the terms of this agreement with the EU, Turkey can make some external trade agreements but its external tariffs must be in line with those within the EU. When the EU makes a trade agreement with a third country, then Turkey must provide access to its markets on the same terms but does not have reciprocal rights of access to the markets of the third country; those have to be negotiated separately.

[11] HM Government (2016) *Alternatives to membership.*
[12] Shepherd and Wedderburn (2016) 'Brexit: The Turkish Model', www. shepwedd.com/sites/default/files/Turkish_Model_Brexit.pdf?_ga=1.24210 0102.568613974.1477908185

Turkey makes no contribution to the EU's budget but is eligible to receive funding as a candidate country. It has no role in EU decision making.

The debate about the potential suitability of Turkey's position is related to the wider consideration of the potential of the UK's main membership of the EU being through the customs union. In a customs union, tariffs are removed for trade between members and there are common external tariffs with third countries outside the union. This is in comparison with a free trade area where there are no internal tariffs but all external trade agreements are negotiated individually. In a free trade area, there need to be checks on the origin of goods to ensure that they have not been routed through free trade members from third countries. The benefits of a customs union are that goods trade freely within it and there are fewer administrative checks across borders within the union.

Both Norway and Switzerland are outside the customs union but do most of their trade with countries within it and have border controls. An initial assessment of the operation of such an approach in the UK has identified operational issues at the ports that would require new customs/border control facilities. In some ports that are short of land capacity providing land for these facilities may be difficult if not impossible to find.

European Grouping for Territorial Cooperation: the British-Irish Council model

The EU's European Groupings of Territorial Cooperation (EGTC) were set up to facilitate and promote cross border working between and within EU member states. They are legally empowered through Regulation (EC) No 1082/2006, based on Article 175 of the Treaty on the Functioning of the European Union (TFEU) updated by Regulation (EU) No 1302/2013 which permitted third states, outside the EU to be members of EGTCs.[13]

[13] Article 1 (4) EU REG 1302/2103; Department for Business Innovation & Skills (2015) 'European Groupings of Territorial Cooperation (EGTC):

EGTC are generally established where there is a land border between states. They have been used for services and projects which have received EU funding and others that have not. These projects and services include transport, health and common initiatives to promote the area.

EGTCs are legal entities set up to facilitate cross border, transnational or interregional cooperation in the EU. They allow regional and local authorities (but also national authorities in smaller or centralised countries) and other public undertakings from different member countries to set up groupings with a legal personality to deliver joint services but are prohibited from some activities such as policing. They can hold and spend joint budgets.

Within the UK, eligible bodies can belong to EGTCs with other member states within the current EU legislation. However, post Brexit, one consideration is the role of EGTCs in maintaining links between the whole or parts of the UK with the EU. At present the EU Regulation requires that this should be with two member states. Post Brexit, the UK has a potential arrangement through the British-Irish Council that could allow for an EGTC to be set up through Ireland although another member may be required unless there is a change in the EU's legislation to accommodate the UK's position.

The major issue with the potential offered by the establishment of an EGTC is how far its legal basis will stretch to include working relationships between the UK and EU. Some of the issues where there may be continuing relationships including major transport policy and networks, environment, energy networks and other infrastructure provision could all be managed within an EGTC framework. What is less clear is the potential of an EGTC to deal with financial services regulations and passporting that would allow banks and other financial services to remain in the UK while operating across and within EU legislation.

Guidance', www.gov.uk/government/uploads/system/uploads/attachment_data/file/448758/BIS-15-290-european-groupings-of-territorial-cooperation-guidance.pdf

As a member of an EGTC, the UK would have no right of representation or ability to contribute to the debates of the EU directly although it could make its views known through the host EU member state – in this case Ireland. However, any such approaches would depend on the willingness of Ireland to engage in discussion on specific issues and then passing on UK views into the EU institutions including the Council of Ministers, European Parliament and EC.

EU neighbourhood policy: the arm's length model

The European Neighbourhood and Partnership Instrument (ENPI) is a foreign policy initiative that promotes cooperation and economic integration between the EU and partner countries which might be member countries at some point in the future. Current neighbourhood countries include Algeria, Armenia, Azerbaijan, Belarus, Egypt, Georgia, Israel, Jordan, Lebanon, Libya, Moldova, Morocco, the Palestinian Authority, the Russian Federation, Syria, Tunisia and Ukraine. It supports partnerships encouraging good governance and social and economic development. Included are 14 cross border cooperation programmes that operate along EU external borders. Neighbourhood countries generally have to agree a range of governance reforms that are included within an Action Plan. In return these countries may be offered access to some of the EU's markets and direct support for improvements.

The UK could develop a neighbourhood agreement with the EU that would be specially tailored to the relationship that is negotiated following the triggering of Article 50. At present the neighbourhood agreements allow the expenditure of funds by the EU in neighbourhood countries. The neighbourhood policy approach would be rather clunky as a means of maintaining links but it would not be impossible. The issue would be whether it provides any advantages over other potential models that are available including those listed here.

Micro state: the tailored model

The micro states of Europe – San Marino, Monaco and Andorra – have specific relationships with the EU and are not part of the EEA. There have been discussions about whether the micro states should have relationships with the EU through membership of EFTA or the EEA but this has not resulted in any practical outcome so the micro states have specific agreements for issues such as trade and Schengen for movement of people with the EU.

The current position of the micro states in relation to the EU is shown in Table 3.2.

Table 3.2: The EU and its working relationships with micro states

Micro state	Euro	Schengen	Single market	Customs union	Council of Europe	OECD
San Marino	yes	yes via Italy	no	yes	yes	yes
Liechtenstein		yes	yes	yes via EEA	yes	yes
Monaco	yes	yes via France	partial	yes via France	yes	yes
The Vatican	yes	yes via Italy	no		yes	
Andorra	yes	via Schengen area	no	yes	yes	yes
Jersey	no	no	yes	yes	no	no but spec agreements
Guernsey	no	no			no	
Isle of Man	no	no			no	
Gibraltar	no		yes	no		

EU enclaves model

In addition to the micro states, the EU also works with nine enclaves. These are areas that are under the jurisdiction of one member state but their geography is entirely land locked within another state and includes a part of Germany that is landlocked in Switzerland.[14]

[14] Vitaliev, V. (2008) *Passport to Enclavia: Travels in Search of a European Identity*, Reportage Press.

Would the EU's approach to enclaves assist areas of the UK that wish to remain in the EU? This seems unlikely in this form unless parts of the UK detached and then aligned with another member state.

The reverse Greenland model

Greenland is an autonomous territory within the Kingdom of Denmark and was a member of the EU between 1973–82. Following a referendum, Greenland opted to change its status to that of an associated overseas territory within the EU. Greenland is eligible for specific funding from the EU's general budget through the EU-Greenland Partnership and the President of the Commission (on behalf of the EU), the Prime Minister of Denmark and the Greenland Premier signed on 19 March 2015 'an umbrella' framework document for the post-2013 Greenland relations, a 'Joint Declaration on relations between the European Union, on the one hand, and the Government of Greenland and the Government of Denmark, on the other'. In this case Greenland was transferred to the category of overseas dependencies and territories.

This approach has been suggested as an option for the UK. It would not require the triggering of Article 50 and would allow Scotland, London, Northern Ireland and Gibraltar to remain within the EU and for other areas to have an associated status.

Although this approach may seem difficult to attain, the EU already has differential models for constituent parts of member states including within the UK where there are special arrangements for the Channel Islands and the Isle of Man as crown dependencies.[15]

---

[15]   Gad, U.P. (2016) 'Could a 'reverse Greenland' arrangement keep Scotland and Northern Ireland in the EU?', LSE EUROPP blog, 7 July, http://blogs.lse.ac.uk/europpblog/2016/07/07/reverse-greenland-arrangement/

Tailored trade agreements: US, Canada and Australia model

In this model, the UK would agree trade terms with the EU for goods and services on the acceptance of EU regulations and payment of a fee. The Canadian model has taken seven years to negotiate and its signature was delayed by the Belgian region of Wallonia before it was finally signed on 30 October 2016. The Canadian agreement (CETA) is primarily focused on specific goods rather than services and rests on the acceptance of the EU's regulations before there is access to its market. The EU is also progressing similar bespoke trade agreements with the US through TTIP and with Australia. The TTIP arrangement is more wide ranging than CETA and includes services. It is being opposed by a number of member states whose governments are opposed to the current version of TTIP and may not be agreed following the election of President Trump. The Australian negotiations are not so far developed.

WTO: the free trade model

The UK is a member of the WTO in its own right although recent negotiations with the WTO have been undertaken on behalf of all EU members by the EC. Initially this arrangement was at the UK's suggestion although there have been subsequent disagreements about the extent to which the EU can negotiate without seeking member state approval. Once the EU has made trade agreements with the WTO it then determines the ways in which they are put into effect. The compliance with these agreements within the EU member states is undertaken by the EC, which is responsible for this function to the WTO. In some cases, such as agriculture, the EU has negotiated and concluded more favourable agreements for its members than the general agreements and this allows for the EU to provide subsidies within specific sectors that might otherwise be considered to be state aid. This is particularly the case for agriculture where the EU provides subsidies for farmers as rural land managers as part of its rural and environmental policies.

If the UK leaves the EU without an agreement, it will revert to the terms of the WTO, with any specific agreements being based on quotas, beyond which punitive tariffs will be applied. In particular, this would mean a loss of subsidies to UK farmers. The UK would negotiate specific trade agreements with any other country and would do this within the WTO rules. It would have no access to existing trade agreements between the WTO, the EU and other countries. The UK would receive no rebate and no funding for infrastructure projects or cohesion. Other regulatory requirements through the WTO such as for agriculture, services and trade remain.

None of the above: UK federal model

One of the consequences of triggering Article 50 and an agreement by the UK government and/or Parliament to leave the EU could be the break up of the UK. This might mean that Scotland and other nations vote in favour of independence. Another alternative is that the UK could move towards a written constitution and adopt a federal model[16] that would clarify the role of each part of the UK including combined authorities and city regions. This model would be similar to that used in Germany and some other federal states including Canada and the United States.

In the federal model, individual nations within the UK could apply to have some relationship with the EU but would be unlikely to attain full membership unless a reverse Greenland option is pursued. The Scottish First Minister has a stated intention to become the 'successor' state to the UK within the EU. This would be achieved by swapping places with the UK if Scotland becomes fully independent. This approach is based on advice from Professor John Curtice of Strathclyde University. He argues that this would be a choice that would face the

---

[16] Brown, G. (2016) 'Extracts from Gordon Brown's speech to the Fabian Society', 3 November, http://gordonandsarahbrown.com/2016/11/gordon-brown-proposes-uk-peoples-constitutional-convention/

EU about keeping Scotland within the EU.[17] This position is based on advice from the Foreign Office on the referendum in 2014 but it may also depend on whether Scotland has voted to leave the UK prior to the Brexit negotiations, as set out in Article 50, having been concluded.

Other UK nations may then also decide to follow the same path, although this approach does not deal with the issues for London.

Remain on status quo terms

The UK remains a full member of the EU until it concludes the exit process through Article 50. There has also been some discussion about whether, even if triggered, Article 50 has to be concluded if both parties agree. The UK may also seek to revoke its request to trigger Article 50 and not proceed with its application to leave the EU. Former Prime Minister Tony Blair has argued that this may occur if the terms offered for leaving are the same as the UK has now or the economic effects posed by leaving the EU emerge in ways that are devastating for the country and the country changes its mind.[18]

Discussion

The variety of options and models that have been set out in this chapter are not exhaustive and each has subtleties that could be developed and exploited as part of negotiation. However, it is possible to reach a number of conclusions. The first is that the range of models is flexible enough for any agreement to be achieved between the EU and the UK. The intentions behind the negotiations are the most important here and both sides will want to explore the aspirations of the other side. The experience and practices of the EU suggest a degree of pragmatism and flexibility through the use of existing or

---

[17] www.barrheadnews.com/news/14831876.__39_Independent_Scotland_could_remain_in_the_EU_after_Brexit_as_successor_state_to_UK__39_/

[18] Tony Blair in an interview with Jason Cowley, *New Statesman*, 25 November 2016, pp 22–9.

new mechanisms that will make any agreement work in the way that the consenting parties wish.

The main issue will be the position of the UK and where it sits on the continuum from remaining in to being completely outside the EU. While the hard Brexit lobby and some of the national press are arguing for a quick and full break between the UK and the EU, actions on the part of the government for the financial services and automotive industries suggest the UK approach that is emerging. For financial services, there have been reassurances that they will retain their rights to passporting: being able to offer financial services in EU member states together with three members of the EEA. If no agreement on passporting can be achieved through Brexit negotiations, then the UK will be in the same position as Switzerland and will need to negotiate specific trading arrangements for financial services. The other option is that the UK could be entirely outside the passporting area. In this case financial services located in London may relocate all or part of their business within the EU to maintain their access to member state markets. The Swiss banks have followed this option.

In another statement, the government has provided reassurances to Nissan and other parts of the automotive industries to suggest that there is an intention to stay within the customs union, although the Prime Minister has since rejected this assumption. The government may seek to introduce elements of reassurance to other sectors of the economy through the Government's Industrial Strategy launched in January 2017. On the other hand, a study by remain supporters has demonstrated that all sectors in the UK economy benefit from EU membership so it would be difficult for the government to differentiate between them.[19]

However, notwithstanding this, providing reassurances and/or financial assistance to any company within the UK falls within the

---

[19] Mason, R. and Wintour, P. (2016) 'Hard Brexit would damage 'almost every sector' of UK economy', *Guardian*, 28 November, www.theguardian.com/ politics/2016/nov/28/hard-brexit-would-damage-almost-every-sector-of-uk-economy

provision of WTO agreements. As operated by the EU, these assurances would constitute state aid: providing some or all companies or sectors with guarantees that would give them competitive and comparative advantages above those from other member states. Further, provisions of state aid do not disappear once the UK leaves the EU but remain part of the UK's treaty obligations with the WTO. Thus the statements of support to different sectors do not seem to fit within the UK's obligations as a trading nation. The resulting confusion on the UK's position and understanding of its agreements within and outside the EU suggest a lack of understanding of commitments and requirements within global agreements that cannot be easily understood.

FOUR

What immediate actions does the UK need to take?

Introduction

Since the referendum on membership of the EU, some of the most difficult issues to consider have been the immediate as well as the longer-term implications of the UK's position both internally and on the wider international stage. There are immediate risks that have to be managed in ways which ensure that the UK is not weakened financially and politically so that it is able to negotiate from a position of strength. These include the stabilisation of the economy and opening arrangements for trade with other states, even though none can be formally started until the UK leaves the EU.

Before the referendum, the UK was the fifth largest global trading nation. The fall in the value of the pound since the referendum now means that the UK has dropped to eighth position. The dependency of the UK's economy on financial services, particularly as being an attractive location for global financial institutions to be housed inside the EU, provides another risk following the referendum. Will financial services companies still want to locate inside the UK and will those here move all or part of their operations elsewhere to ensure that they are able to continue operating within the EU?

In addition to the immediate requirement to stabilise the UK economy, there are other areas where the government needs to signal its position to calm the country. The first is to identify the UK's position in the negotiations with the EU – that is to identify which of the options available will be the dominant mode and desired outcome. The UK government has argued that this position should remain confidential while the negotiations are taking place. This has led to charges that the Prime Minister is putting the future stability of the Conservative Party ahead of the needs of the country. Businesses represented through organisations like the CBI (Confederation of British Industry) have also requested that the government's position and objectives are clarified. They fear a loss of investment the longer this period of uncertainty continues. However, the range of potential outcomes for the UK (as set out in Chapter Three) are not only economic but are also each accompanied by highly politically charged positions that attach each model to a particular Brexit camp. Further, although the pro Brexit campaign stated that there would be no need to leave the single market if the UK left the EU, they and the Prime Minister are now arguing that this was the outcome of the referendum and that there should be a complete break with the EU on all matters. It has become clear that wider public engagement in the discussions represents both interests and concerns about the selection of a specific approach and what it might mean. It is now recognised that the differences between the negotiating positions are so significant that they need to have some wider airing before the government proceeds.

The issues related to EU membership, including whether the UK will be part of the single market, the customs union, the free trade area, the EEA or some other bespoke arrangement, lead to a range of implications. These will be considered as part of a full package of relationships in the negotiations on the terms of agreement reached within the discussions after Article 50 is triggered. However, there are some issues that need to be addressed more immediately and cannot wait for the outcome of ten or more years of discussion or transitional arrangements or wrangling and this chapter considers some of these. Positions vary on the matter of existing EU citizens that are currently resident and working in the UK. There is also a need to consider issues relating to immediate labour force requirements as uncertainty about longer-term employment status could encourage EU citizens to find other jobs elsewhere, particularly those with high levels of skills and training.

Finally, there is a need for the government to address the level of economic and social disconnection that many people feel, particularly in England, and how this might be addressed in a more fundamental way. The US election has shown that the Brexit vote may have been part of a wider popularist resistance to the outcomes of globalisation and trade liberalisation in communities where no new jobs have been located or grown. The UK government has to address this level of anger despite what happens in negotiations with the EU. The stabilisation of these economic and outsider concerns might also be fundamental in achieving agreement and resolution within the UK on the future relations with the EU.

Stabilise markets

The most important economic outcome of the referendum result has been an effective 11–16% devaluation of the pound. This has required the Bank of England to take measures to retain economic confidence in the UK's currency, including quantitative easing. In practical terms the drop in the value of sterling is a benefit to those exporting their goods aboard as they are effectively cheaper than they were, although this has not yet been demonstrated in practice when the trade gap has widened rather than reduced.[1] It is also a benefit to tourists and may increase the number of visitors in the coming period, although this has not emerged immediately other than visits across the Irish border.

However, there are also negative impacts of a loss of the value of the pound. The first is that the costs of imports will increase. Where

---

[1] Office for National Statistics (2016) 'Statistical bulletin: UK trade: Sept 2016', www.ons.gov.uk/economy/nationalaccounts/balanceofpayments/bulletins/uktrade/sept2016

imports are 'spot' or short-term priced such as petrol, increased costs are felt more rapidly although this might be slightly offset by low prices in the international oil market. For other goods it may take longer for these prices to increase. This will occur where pricing has been agreed as part of future orders or where the price has been hedged or guaranteed for a period. This will apply to foodstuffs and could apply to other goods that are regularly imported but of variable supply. For other goods that are imported or for travel overseas, prices are immediately increased and since the referendum there have been periods where exchange rates have offered pound to Euro parity. This may discourage UK citizens from foreign travel or they may change their destinations. The effect of this devaluation in the value of the pound will affect all but domestic destinations.

If imported goods, raw materials and food stuffs are increased in price then the manufacturers and retailers have a choice as to whether they pass on the price rises to customers and consumers or to contain them within their business. In practice it will be hard to contain 15% and there are forecasts that there will be price rises in 2017 and beyond. This is likely to cause inflation and a pressure on consumers for higher salaries to pay for these rises in their cost of living. If pay increases are not forthcoming, then standards of living will fall and are likely to affect those on the lowest incomes who spend the greatest proportion of their budget on food and energy.

Although there were predictions of an economic meltdown for the UK following a leave vote in the referendum, the Governor of the Bank of England has remarked that consumers have not witnessed these price increases immediately. Indeed, price pressure has remained downward as retailers have overstocked and consumer competition together with action from the regulators are maintaining or reducing prices. Inflation reduced slightly in October 2016 but this has been ascribed to retailers trying to improve sales before public financial anxiety about rising prices set in and has increased subsequently.

In the medium term, one of the major concerns for the damaging potential of inflation is that many people have not lived through a period where this has been an issue. The last period of serious inflation and downward pay pressures was in the early 1990s when there were high levels of credit card defaults, negative equity in housing and economic slowdown. Since then, the banks have been required to be more watchful about household credit card use and mortgage payments but nevertheless these issues are still outside the experience of many. County court judgements for credit default have risen in 2016.

Overall, a rise in inflation has some positive benefits to the national economy as it helps to effectively reduce historic debts and repayments but the triple lock on pensioners' incomes also means that pensions will be increased in line with inflation. This provides some increase in spending power but will not support those in work on low pay. There will also be issues about whether minimum and living wages can be increased fast enough to keep up with inflation.

What can the government do about this in addition to the measures taken by the Bank of England? The first action to stabilise the pound is to have a clear view about the form that Brexit will take, as the markets respond poorly to uncertainty. This has been compounded by the election of Trump in the US and the expected changes in the relative fortunes of US stock and bond markets. On the day that the High Court handed down its judgement in how Article 50 can be triggered, the pound increased by 1.5%, although this is in the context of a long running decline in value since 23 June. Second, the government could commit to supporting less long-term state expenditure through non-austerity means. In this case, there could be focus on prevention in health and retrofitting of building stock to reduce the expenditure on energy for businesses and householders. There could also be more investment in local provision of energy to reduce energy supply costs. In housing, the market may slow down to reduce prices and there could be increased landlord regulation and improved security of tenure in the rented market. The Uber judgement will also serve to regulate the gig economy and give rights to those working on zero hours contracts. The Matthew Taylor review of employment rights and zero hours contracts could also provide more stability to those who may be increasingly marginalised in an uncertain economic climate.

Reinvent welfare state to re-unify country

While there are many discussions about the causes of the UK vote to leave the EU, the scale of the vote to leave in England needs to be considered in more depth not least because it was symptomatic of fissures in English society. This disruption will need a response from government whatever future for the UK is negotiated with the EU as a result of invoking Article 50. Some have attributed the vote to the rise of global popularism that has also been evident in the US presidential election in 2016. This removal of trust in government has been attributed to the effects of globalisation and neo-liberal policies applied by governments that are run by metropolitan elites. It is also ascribed to an anti-urban mood but is also characteristic of cities and towns that have been de-industrialised over a long period of time. As with the movement that backs Trump in the US, there appears to be a feeling of separation shared by many people who believe that they have been left behind and forgotten about by governments, have lost their jobs, have little investment in training or transport and are just getting by. There is resentment against those who appear to be located in islands of fast growth and high wealth having an increasing disregard for those stranded elsewhere.

This lack of trust represents a breakdown in the post-1945 consensus that has characterised western democracies. The welfare state in England has become increasingly undermined and destabilised in comparison with other parts of the UK and the EU. The austerity programme run by the UK government over 2010–16 served to undermine the lives of those who have been on low incomes or in need for years. While the Labour government committed to increase NHS spending to average levels in other OECD countries of 11%, from the current level of 8%, there are no Government commitments for this now.

In 2016, Theresa May referred to the need to rebuild the welfare state in her speech following her appointment as Conservative Party leader and Prime Minister, although many commentators suggested that this is a speech that all prime ministers make but not many deliver. Is this the case with Theresa May and how far is this linked to rebuilding the country after the schism of the referendum? In finding her texts for reform, it appears that May has returned to the 1940s. Her first announcement was about the reintroduction of grammar schools into the English education system, with the explanation that these would be available to those on the lowest incomes as well as those whose children currently populate the country's elite schools in the state, intermediate and private sectors. This proposal has been met with howls of derision from all sides and may be voted down in Parliament but May was trying to demonstrate an escape route of hope for those who remain stuck in poverty and who have been left behind.

Her second set of actions appears to be focusing on the five evils identified by Beveridge in 1942. These were squalor, ignorance, want, idleness and disease. The creation of the welfare state that served to deliver the military covenant after the Second World War, but also to deal with the social conditions of the 1930s, addressed each of these evils by focusing on the provision of housing and giving insurance against uncertainty. This was primarily a national programme and set of entitlements. However, post-devolution in 1999, the welfare state has been eroded specifically in England, particularly through the austerity programme 2010–16 that not only cut the budget of local authorities that operate on the front line of meeting need but also legislated to reduce the certainties in council house tenancy, financial support for the disabled and those who are chronically ill. The earnings cap and welfare trap levels also changed.

During this period, many people became reliant on food banks. This was also a period of increased uncertainty for employees. Many more people were working on zero hours contracts with no employment rights or benefits. In localities that had deindustrialised in the Thatcher period following the miners' strike, communities have been dependent on welfare benefits since, and had not felt any uplift in the economy in comparison with London.[2] In these cases, there was also a feeling that

[2]   Elliott, L. (2016) 'Half UK budget deficit is "down to job destruction in older industrial areas"', *Guardian*, 6 November, www.theguardian.com/

after the economic crash in 2007, no one in the banking sector had been made to pay for the subsequent recession. It was this recession that also encouraged more migrants from the EU into the UK, where jobs were still available. However, in some communities where those on benefits had been arguing that they were unable to get a job, their position was undercut by eastern European migrants who were able to find jobs that they were willing to do.

This undermining of social cohesion in England, particularly in places that had a stagnant economy and little ethnic diversity led to a blame culture that was encouraged by the press. The pressure on the NHS was not seen to be as a result of management or funding but rather due to an increase in migrants. Places that had been underinvested and were peripheral in terms of access by public transport – particularly on the east coast – blamed migration for the sense of frustration that they felt and started to support UKIP. All of these areas – whether urban, coastal or rural – felt left behind and blaming this on a metropolitan elite. They found the leave campaign echoed their emotions and they wanted to make a protest.

Another group in favour of Brexit was from the old Commonwealth who were of the view that in-migration from the EU was preventing their families being able to get visas to relocate to Britain. By voting leave, they thought that the subsequent labour shortages that the UK would be likely to experience could be filled in the same ways as they were in the 1950s and this was particularly the case for those from the Indian sub-continent.

The divide in England that has been exposed by the UK referendum may take generations to heal but government action to support those feeling vulnerable and left behind is required to repair social relations and a sense of cohesion. A new social and economic covenant is

business/2016/nov/06/half-of-uk-deficit-is-result-of-job-destruction-in-older-industrial-areas; Beatty, C. and Fothergill, S. (2016) *Jobs, Welfare and Austerity*, Centre for Regional Economic and Social Research at Sheffield Hallam University, www4.shu.ac.uk/research/cresr/sites/shu.ac.uk/files/cresr30th-jobs-welfare-austerity.pdf

required in England regardless of Brexit, although achieving Brexit has become the point of focus or test for this commitment to English people. Some commentators have argued that this points to the need for greater devolution in England so that local authorities can be more responsive to specific local issues and be provided with the powers and the means to support local people and develop their future. The UK is the most centralised country in the OECD and despite the rhetoric of devolution this position has not changed at the local level.

The lack of cohesion in society since the referendum has also been marked by an increase in racial hate crimes and casual abuse that have been reported to the police. People have been abused in public transport, shops have been torched and there have been deaths of migrants and an MP in favour of remain. Some of the work to repair this cohesion has already begun, including the Matthew Taylor review of employment rights for those on zero hours contracts, which have been strengthened by the judgement on the employment status of Uber drivers. This found that they were not self employed nor employees but fell into a new and emerging group of workers that had some entitlements and for whom the employing company had some responsibilities in term of taxation and national insurance payments. The processes through which the disabled and chronically ill were assessed before they could be given benefits have also been rolled back. The right to buy of some housing association properties has been stopped. The welfare trap is also being considered while a House of Commons Select Committee has argued that the need for the pensioners' triple lock on pension increases, put in place because pensioners were financially disadvantaged in comparison with other groups, is now no longer required as pensioners have caught up. It is children now who need the most financial support. All these small things will not make the differences required to repair the social fabric and cohesion of England, although they are necessary first steps.

Consider labour markets and skills

In 2000, the UN proposed that migration might be a means of addressing falling populations including in the countries of the EU that would have shrinking populations by 2020.[3] In 2001, the OECD found that the costs of ageing populations would be a key issue where working age populations were in concurrent decline.[4] The first country not to replace its population through its birth rate and in-migration was Italy in 1995[5] and the last would have been the UK in 2019 with all other EU states appearing on this list in the intervening period. Declining populations are a cause for concern in a number of ways. First, a low birth rate does not provide states with sufficient labour to grow its economy and where there are labour shortages there can be wage inflation and higher prices. Second, an older demographic profile means that there are fewer young people to generate the taxes required to support them in addition to the rest of the economy. Third, a deficit in the labour market means that a state is more dependent on the skills of economic migrants and some of its population may find more attractive jobs elsewhere particularly if, like the UK, the population deficit occurred towards the end of this period and after that of other states.

In response to these issues, the opportunities provided by the EU accession states to support the labour market after 2004 were taken by the UK government. It could have chosen to restrict the migration from A8 countries[6] for a period of time but decided rather that it would

[3] United Nations (2000) 'New report on replacement migration issued by UN Population division', Press release DEV/2234, POP/735, 17 March, www.un.org/press/en/2000/20000317.dev2234.doc.html

[4] Visco, I. (2001) 'Ageing populations: economics issues and policy challenges', Economic Policy for Ageing Societies Conference, 18–19 June, www.oecd.org/economy/growth/2431724.pdf

[5] www.un.org/esa/population/publications/migration/italy.pdf

[6] The eight eastern European countries that acceded to the EU in 2014 were the Czech Republic, Estonia, Hungary, Latvia, Lithuania, Poland, Slovakia and Slovenia. Malta and Cyprus joined the Union at the same time.

open the country to in-migrants. There was an expectation that the UK would be particularly attractive to skilled people from Poland, which already had a long and positive link to the UK with established post-war Polish communities in a number of cities. This policy was seen as a way to ensure that skills that were difficult to obtain in the UK including in construction would be available to boost housebuilding and development. Initially many skilled male migrants came to the UK leaving their families at home and remitting funds but over time younger Poles also started to come to the UK, with many young women entering the social and child care sectors. The UK birth rate started to increase as these migrants started families and by 2011 there were Polish people in every part of the UK. There have also been concerns that in-migrants have been a cause of housing shortages and increased property prices despite other contributory factors, such as a lack of a successful government policy for all tenures.

The downturn in the economies of EU states after the economic crash in 2007 also meant that Eurozone countries had high levels of unemployment. As the UK was the only EU economy that was growing it became an attractive place for young people (particularly those from Spain and Italy) to find a job. The same was true for older and more professionally qualified people from France and Germany and, in 2012, London was said to be the equivalent of the sixth largest French city.[7] Although there were no jobs for these people at home, some countries, like Germany, began to worry about a brain drain and their own shrinking populations. The refugee crisis allowed Germany to take more migrants to start to support its economy in the longer term. Although all these emigration waves have some positive effects on the economies of the EU and the UK they have brought resentment and opposition from older populations. Some countries like Italy and Greece have borne a major burden of migrants finding their way to Europe and trying to get to the UK, which is still acting as a labour magnet.

[7]   Ash, L. (2012) 'London, France's sixth biggest city', BBC News Magazine, 30 May, www.bbc.co.uk/news/magazine-18234930

As the UK discusses its post–Brexit future in the world, the issue about labour force and inflation may return. In some sectors such as health, 10% of doctors and 4% of nurses – in total 55,000 staff – are from the EU.[8] There are concerns that they may not stay in the longer term if there are no guarantees about free movement of labour and as economies improve there will be jobs at home. A second sector to be affected will be universities where 17% of employees – 32,000 academics – are from the EU.[9] Universities are already working directly with their EU staff to establish a legal means of staying in the UK in the longer term. In other areas such as financial services, the French and German professionals living primarily in London may hope that their employing companies will need to relocate inside the EU to maintain passporting so they will be able to move back home as part of the diminishing role of the UK in these sectors. Other areas of the economy that will be hit by falling migration or return home will be social care, construction, retail and the heritage and tourism sectors. These reductions may not matter if the UK has enough labour force with the right skills to fill these voids that will be left. The industrial strategy launched in 2017[10] will need to demonstrate how the future UK labour market may work. In some cases, it may mean a greater number of migrants from Ireland who have been going further afield to Canada and Australia to find jobs since 2007 and will not be affected by any changes in citizenship post Brexit.

In the short term, the government will need to find a way to prevent high and continuing labour shortages that will drive up pay. Most public sector bodies are more effective than they were the last time this problem occurred in the 1970s so although there might be some further scope for efficiencies and digitalisation this might not be adequate to

---

[8] Full Fact (2016) 'EU immigration and NHS staff', https://fullfact.org/immigration/immigration-and-nhs-staff/

[9] Henley, J., Kirchgaessner, S. and Oltermann, P. (2016) 'Brexit fears may see 15% of UK university staff leave, group warns', *Guardian*, 25 September, www.theguardian.com/education/2016/sep/25/brexit-may-force-15-of-staff-at-uk-universities-to-leave-warns-group

[10] www.gov.uk/government/consultations/building-our-industrial-strategy

cope with staff losses. In all personal services including care for the increasingly elderly population, transport provision and education and child care of a growing population, there may be considerable labour market shortages to confront. However, potentially as an unintended outcome of the referendum, the growth of EU migrants to the UK was at very high rates in the quarter following the referendum. Many EU citizens may be deciding to come to the UK while it remains a member. At the same time, the UK economy is growing and unemployment is reducing so these in-migrants are being placed into the economy and mitigating rises in wage costs due to labour shortages.

Stabilise existing projects and programmes

While the UK government has stated that it will both guarantee funding for projects that have been agreed until the UK leaves the EU and that it will use the provisions of Article 50 to maintain EU legislation following a UK departure from the EU there are some questions about major projects that remain unresolved. These projects fall primarily in two main groups. The first comprises transport projects that form part of the Trans European Networks (TEN-T)[11] and the Sustainable Urban Mobility Plans (SUMPs).[12] The second group is concerned with the €50 billion worth of projects that have been funded by the European Investment Bank (EIB). The latter group will continue their funding relationship with the EIB until the loans are paid back but the former group of transport and some energy projects may be more problematic.

The major group of individual TEN-T transport projects have been approved under EU legislation stretching back to 1996. This is when the major transport proposals to provide links between all parts of the EU, including the accession states, started. TEN-T

---

[11] http://ec.europa.eu/transport/infrastructure/tentec/tentec-portal/site/index_en.htm, www.europarl.europa.eu/atyourservice/en/displayFtu.html?ftuId=FTU_5.8.1.html

[12] www.eltis.org/mobility-plans

comprises of transport corridors that were designated across the EU and comprised of at least three modes in each corridor. In order to support the improvement of these networks, the EU provided some financial support towards design and implementation costs. Following the 1996 Regulation, there were amendments and some changes but largely these have been delivered. In the UK these networks included HS1, Crossrail, the West Coast rail upgrade and the A14.[13] There were improvements to surface travel links to airports across the UK in order to comply with EU agreements on reduction in car access and also major work at mainline railway stations to make them more attractive to potential travellers. The last major reset of this policy was in 2013 when new Trans European Networks were agreed and were more focused on north–south links compared with the earlier east–west focus. Here the projects that are included are HS2, cross rail, the northern rail hub and improving transport links in south Wales.[14]

Since 2013 a second range of policies to improve transport within functional economic areas in cites and sub-regions has been added through SUMPs. Through this, public transport within FEAs[15] can be improved with EU funding to improve access, integrated multi modal travel using smart cards and digital information systems to improve the traveller's journey choices. These SUMPs were launched in Bristol and each FEA in the UK is preparing a programme.

Other major infrastructure projects have also been supported through EU programmes including major projects for energy although the Trans European Networks programme for energy (TEN-E)[16] has yet to be agreed and member states are working together on an Energy

[13] www.gov.uk/government/publications/trans-european-network-transport-ten-t-programme

[14] https://ec.europa.eu/transport/node/4876

[15] Functional Economic Areas http://webarchive.nationalarchives.gov.uk/20120919132719/http:/www.communities.gov.uk/documents/localgovernment/pdf/1469713.pdf

[16] https://ec.europa.eu/energy/en/topics/infrastructure, www.gov.uk/government/uploads/system/uploads/attachment_data/file/311184/uk_manual_procedures_ten_e_regulation.pdf

Europe programme. This has supported major project such as Hinkley Point. In terms of funding, the Juncker major infrastructure funding scheme that was launched in 2014 has also supported many UK projects including those for hospitals and the UK has been one of the highest beneficiaries of these funds. However, the inclusion of a proposal to leave EURATOM as part of the Bill to trigger Article 50 may also have effects on existing nuclear projects.[17]

The legal underpinning of these infrastructure projects rests in the treaties and is supported by the principles of social, economic and territorial cohesion. Their environmental aspects are supported by the EU application and implementation of the UN agreements on climate change and the role of the single market policies in reducing locational disparities and increasing competitiveness across the EU's territory.

In the event of Brexit, the UK government will be able to transpose the relevant legislation, although the link between this and the founding EU treaties that will be removed may need to be addressed by specific legislation. The longer-term relationships between the EU and UK will need infrastructure projects and linkages to support the UK's economy both internally and externally. The funding support that these major projects attract will have to be replaced if they are to continue. It is unknown whether any UK government savings on EU contributions will be directed towards these projects in the future when they are not supported through EU legislation. UK politicians may decide that funding should be provided for different projects and airport linkages to non-EU trading partners may be deemed to be more important than improving rail and short sea shipping routes across the EU.

If the UK were staying in the EU, then it would also now be developing the comprehensive networks within the UK that fill in the TEN-T spaces. The EU has agreed that these will be defined by 2030 and implemented by 2050. Although the UK may not be participating in this programme it will need to consider the effects of

---

[17] www.theguardian.com/business/2017/jan/27/uk-exit-eu-atomic-treaty-brexit-euratom-hinkley-point-c

the support for these transport movements across the mainland of the EU and its potential impact on competitiveness and pricing within the single market, customs union and free trade area.

Prepare negotiating positions

The Prime Minister outlined her negotiating objectives in a speech on 17 January 2017 which included a full UK exit from the EU including the single market and customs union although her stated aim is to maintain as many trade links with the EU as can be negotiated. There will be some specific decisions to be made that will accompany the process. Charles Grant of the Centre for European Reform has identified six.[18] The first he has described as the divorce settlement – that is dividing up assets and also debts, including pension rights of staff and other existing commitments that have a longer pay back period. This has to be agreed within the two–year period that is set out in Article 50 although it can be extended with the agreement of the UK and the EU.

The second area of negotiation will be to determine what future relationship the UK would like with the EU and how this might be agreed. The options available are set out in Chapter Three and Grant is of the view that the Prime Minister will opt for a free trade area agreement which will deal with tariffs on goods but possibly not on services. It will also exclude non–tariff barriers such as recognition of professional qualifications and regulatory systems. The third area is the need to provide some interim cover for the UK economy in the transition period. If the UK decides to transpose EU legislation as a means of facilitating the transitional period, there will be no anchoring treaties which support the legislation and consequent uncertainty is likely about the way that disputes will be handled. Will these still be heard by the European Court of Justice?

[18] Grant, C. (2016) 'Six Brexit deals that Theresa May must strike', Opinion piece (Prospect), Centre for European Reform, 28 July, www.cer.org.uk/in-the-press/six-brexit-deals-theresa-may-must-strike

On the UK's full and individual membership of the World Trade Organization, this will need to be negotiated and all other 162 members of the WTO will have to agree this. It will take only one country to cause difficulties to slow this down and prevent the UK's full membership of the WTO until this issue is resolved. Another trade issue that has not been considered much in Brexit discussions is that the UK will need to broker individual arrangements with all the countries with which the EU has 52 trade arrangements – on the day of departure from the EU, the UK will lose the benefit of all these deals. The UK will also be seeking new trade deals with those countries where the EU does not have a current deal, but the UK is not able to open negotiations on these until it leaves the EU. Finally, the UK will have to negotiate agreements on defence, security and police issues and judicial cooperation. This might be easier to negotiate, not least with increasing foreign policy concerns to the west and east of Europe and from the US.

While these are the formal processes that have to be considered, other organisations such as IPPR have focused on the binary choice of remaining in the single market and restricting the free movement of European citizens.[19] In its assessment, IPPR considers that the government has six options to consider in relation to what it wishes to achieve on the free movement of EU citizens. The first option is that the UK retains the status quo and allows free movement to continue. This option could be arrived at by negotiation or by the UK deciding not to invoke Article 50. The second option is that free movement could only apply to workers and would need to be approved through pre-agreed job offers.

The third option is that free movement continues but with the addition of an emergency break if certain points on a pre-agreed set of criteria are met. The fourth option is the free movement for some workers who are priority requirements for the UK labour

[19] Morris, M. (2016) 'Beyond free movement? Six possible futures for the UK's EU migration policy', IPPR, 13 July, www.ippr.org/publications/where-next-for-free-movement

force together with free movement for students, family members and retirees. The fifth option is to introduce comprehensive labour migrant movements in ways that are similar to those for non-EU citizens at the moment. The last option is to introduce a visa system for all EU citizens entering the UK.

Each of these options would have a differential impact on the UK economy but those in favour of a hard Brexit would probably advocate one of the last three options. Those who favour a more open labour market would be more likely to favour the first three, which are more aligned with any likely continuing UK access to the single market. However, as IPPR points out, these options also may not be considered to meet the terms of the referendum result and to be morally and politically unacceptable.

There is also another issue to consider on the terms of the UK departure from the EU and that is whether the negotiations to leave the EU are being led by the Prime Minister in order to serve the wider interests of the country or whether they are driven by Conservative Party political interests. The Prime Minister's failure to reveal or discuss the government's preferred outcome from this process has brought her under increasing pressure. The first pressure is from the legal challenges, particularly the successful challenge to the High Court for Parliament to be involved in triggering Article 50. This has been determined by the Supreme Court and following pressure from Parliament, the Prime Minister has published a White Paper alongside the Bill that is required to trigger Article 50, and agreed that she will give Parliament a vote on the final terms that are agreed between the UK and the EU. There is also a separate legal challenge about whether invoking Article 50 also triggers Article 127 of the EEA Agreement. Whatever happens, both Houses of Parliament are becoming increasingly disturbed by the lack of open leadership on the UK's position.

The second set of challenges is coming from within the civil service. In a leaked report, prepared by Deloitte as part of its consultancy for the Cabinet Office, fears about lack of direction, the volume and cost of the amount of work commissioned on the effects of Brexit by different government departments and an over centralising prime ministerial style have received attention in the media. In asking whether this leaked report mattered, the BBC's Laura Kuenssberg[20] has argued that it does because it has captured the way everyone on the inside of government is thinking. Another critic has been the Institute for Government, a small organisation set up to work with the civil service. Its representatives have also spoken of this lack of communication inside the civil service both in evidence to the Parliamentary Select Committee on Brexit[21] as well as in their reports and blogs, among which is one entitled 'silence is not a strategy'.[22] Sir Simon Fraser, former head of the Foreign and Commonwealth Office, also set out the challenges being faced by the civil service at the same Parliamentary Select Committee meeting. These concerns about lack of direction and Ministerial competence have also been set out at length in the resignation email of the UK's Ambassador to the EU.[23]

The third set of challenges is coming from business including the City of London and other business bodies that are asking for some indication of the direction of travel so that they can prepare for change. Additionally, the UK's regulatory bodies are requiring financial services companies to prepare for change as part of their risk management practices.

Another set of challenges is coming from the devolved nations who are working together, frequently also including London in order to engage in a debate about their priorities for any future EU–UK arrangements. Despite an early set of meetings between the new Prime

[20] Kuennsberg, L. (2016) 'Does the Brexit memo matter?', BBC News, 15 November, www.bbc.co.uk/news/uk-politics-37986590

[21] Crace, J. (2016) 'A plan for Brexit? Hilary Benn's gameshow draws a blankety blank', *Guardian*, 16 November, www.theguardian.com/politics/2016/nov/16/a-plan-for-brexit-hilary-benns-gameshow-draws-a-blankety-blank

[22] Rutter, J. and White, H. (2016) 'Planning Brexit: silence is not a strategy', Institute for Government, 29 September, www.instituteforgovernment.org.uk/publications/planning-brexit

[23] http://uk.businessinsider.com/full-text-britain-eu-ambassador-sir-ivan-rogers-resignation-letter-brexit-2017-1?r=US&IR=T

Minister and the First Minister of Scotland to provide reassurances, there has been little practical progress on how these arrangements should take place. After some delay, the Prime Minister has established these working arrangements through the Department for Exiting the EU and regular meetings have been put into place, despite the Secretary of State for that department earlier stating that this was a UK government issue and not one for devolved governments. Nevertheless, the First Ministers of Wales and Scotland decided to join the group that argued against the government's appeal to the Supreme Court about the role of Parliament in triggering Brexit.

While there have been criticisms from the governments of Scotland, Wales and Northern Ireland about their role and contribution to the negotiations and agreements, there have also been criticisms by the Institute for Government (IfG) in London. In a report considering the issues of how Brexit should be negotiated within a four nation Britain,[24] it argues that there has to be clear leadership from the Prime Minister about the level of political commitment to this inclusion. Second, it argues that there must be agreements on principles of joint working, including how disagreements will be resolved, and also the importance of the basic principles of transparency and accountability in the process.

Further it states that there should be clarity about stages in the process and what will be agreed when and how this is to be done – suggesting that the three key phases are the agreement of the UK's position, the negotiation period with the EU and then the assessment of the likely final agreement. The IfG argues that although there was no legal requirement in the Referendum Act to take into the account the relative votes in each of the devolved nations and England, as there would be in a federal system such as Canada, since devolution in 1999, Parliament has upheld a principle that it will not normally legislate for the devolved nations unless there is consent in those

[24] Paun, A. and Miller, G. (2016) 'Four-nation Brexit', Institute for Government, 24 October, www.instituteforgovernment.org.uk/publications/four-nation-brexit

areas for the legislation. Where the UK government has argued that a consent motion is not required in relation to Wales, these decisions have been challenged in the courts. This legislative consent process is now recognised in law for Scotland and will soon be legislated for Wales. While the UK government has consistently argued that invoking Article 50 is an international foreign policy issue that is not devolved, relations with the EU are contained in the legislation that established the devolved governments so there will be some effects on their powers and role in any outcome other than remain.

This latter point also needs to include the basis of the devolved settlement with each nation as the UK devolution agreements are anchored by the EU's principle of subsidiarity confirmed in the Treaties of Rome (1957), Maastricht (1992) and Lisbon (2007). Also there needs to be some clarity about what will be devolved following Brexit. The current settlement for the devolved powers primarily relates to the implementation of legislation that the UK had already agreed within the EU. Will the same issues be devolved after Brexit? The EU principles of economic, social and territorial cohesion, also enshrined in these three EU treaties, form the basis for the financial settlement and distribution of funding between the UK, England and the devolved governments. How will devolution work in future and what role will the new directly elected mayors of combined authorities in England, together with London, have on this discussion?

FIVE

Beyond Brexit, what will stay the same?

Overview of key government policies in addition to Brexit

While much of the UK's domestic legislation comes through agreements made in the EU, as noted in Chapter Two, in some cases the EU is acting as an intermediary for member states with global institutions, notably the World Trade Organization (WTO) and the United Nations. In these cases, the treaty agreements are negotiated by the EU on behalf of all member states and once agreed the EU provides both the legal mechanisms for their implementation and manages compliance on behalf of the global body initiating the agreement. Following Brexit, the UK will still be bound into these treaty obligations while compliance will be direct with the initiating organisation. Where the UK wishes to undertake trade in the future, post Brexit, with the EU under any formal agreements – as part of the single market, the customs union or the free trade area – there will still be a need to comply with these requirements and to demonstrate that they have been met as part of the EU's terms of trade with any other country with which it trades as part of an agreement or not.

The UK also has relationships with other international bodies including the World Bank, the International Monetary Fund and the

OECD. The relationships between the EU and the IMF and World Bank are strong but primarily advisory about the relative strengths of member state economies and macroeconomic and fiscal policies that may need to be applied. The OECD is also an international body that provides economic advice to its members and in this case it is related to more detailed policy research and examination of the effects on individual member states. The OECD is engaged in a number of key policy programmes with its members including the negotiation of openness in tax agreements through which it is agreeing bilateral agreements with many smaller states around the world. It is also reviewing tax transparency and tax offshoring, where global companies move their operations to locations that they regard as being most tax beneficial rather than paying taxes in countries where earnings are made.

Another area of OECD policy is concerned with sub-state governance and the alignment of administrative and economic boundaries. This programme has been operational since 2000 and, in 2014, the head of the OECD stated that over half of its member states had now embarked on programmes to realign sub-state administrative boundaries with economic areas. The OECD undertakes its work through direct research but also through country and topic reviews where it examines and compares the performance of individual members against others. It does not particularly examine the EU as a whole, leaving that to the EC, but it does look at the consequences of specific governance arrangements for particular activities including transport, education and skills. These studies rely on the member state inviting the OECD to undertake this work and although they are focused on specific localities, the choice of location and the findings are also expected to have wider applicability acting as a means of policy transfer and mobility. Following Brexit, the OECD may become relatively more important to the UK in its focus and examination of economic and governance policies, and the UK may seek more OECD advice on the assessment of the success of its own policies within a wider international economic environment. This chapter discusses the implications of the relationships between these international organisations and the UK and the potential strength of policies that will remain following the UK's departure from the EU.

Discussion of the May doctrine of new welfarism

As noted earlier, the new May doctrine on welfarism is likely to have an impact on the country's social cohesion but will also have implications for its likely economic success. While the UK was the world's fifth largest economy before the 2016 referendum, it also has lower rankings on productivity and infrastructure provision than its wider cohort in the G7. This lower productivity is partly related to the investment in equipment and the value added that can be achieved through its operation but it also relates to skill levels among the labour force. At present, UK productivity is higher in the south than the north and a recent study has shown that, despite the growth in the economy, the areas which were formerly the locations of heavy industry have been left behind with higher proportions of the population dependent on the range of benefit payments. The May industrial strategy[1] is intended to address some of these issues but it is hard to consider which measures might be most successful. However, it is also in these areas where support for Brexit was highest and the changes in the welfare system brought through austerity have had their most unsettling outcomes.

Policy prescriptions for these areas of welfare dependency are difficult and seem to rely on older forms of intervention including suggestions that companies or government functions are relocated from the south to other parts of England and that companies already located there should be given assurances that will encourage them to remain and invest post Brexit. While not the main focus of UK government activity through the Brexit negotiations, finding solutions to changing the productivity and labour market engagement in these areas will be critical and will be addressed by new sub-regional governance arrangements as discussed later in this chapter. Although the UK had

[1] http://researchbriefings.parliament.uk/ResearchBriefing/Summary/CBP-7682

the lowest level of unemployment since 2011, in October 2016 the jobs that had been filled in the previous quarterly period were primarily by workers from the EU.

While the government's austerity programme has served to vilify those who are dependent on the state, encouraging more into the workplace primarily by cutting benefits, there is still a need for longer-term government intervention and a strategy that will differ from those that have gone before. Some of the solutions will relate to social and economic culture as well as skills and education. Those areas of the country that have lower productivity also have lower levels of new firm start ups particularly by women who are more represented in other areas of the country. A second issue is that many parts of the country where productivity is lower are hard to reach by public transport. People who live there find it expensive and difficult to access work and the severance caused by this poor transport also means that fewer people visit these locations and they can become more socially isolated. Although access to jobs is not the whole answer, the introduction of more systematic availability of buses and improved local railway services could do more to reduce the isolation and improve the attractiveness of these communities where the population is declining and increasingly dependent.

Implications for state devolution

The major thrust for devolution in the UK has primarily come from its nations, notably Scotland and Wales, but it is also important to remember that their case has been supported through the application of the principle of subsidiarity in the Rome, Maastricht and Lisbon treaties. While the principle of devolved nations has now been firmly set within the UK, the development of more documentation within nations has not been so well supported and has been slow to take off. While the loss of the subsidiarity principle to support devolution will be an issue, the principle is also supported by the OECD for economic reasons and is being rolled out across more than half of its members. The OECD favours devolution to functional economic areas as it defines these areas as being the most economically efficient and effective as scales of government for the modern state. It regards these as the most effective for issues such as transport management including public transport customs, they concur with the UN's new urban agenda for a sustainable future[2] and they can provide identifiable leaders who are directly elected and responsible for getting this done. The OECD is also in favour of fiscal federalism where there is a direct link between taxes raised and spent in any locality. This is a particular issue in England where there is considerable centralisation and control over local expenditure with no local taxation in marked contrast with other OECD and EU countries.

While the devolution to this scale has started in England through the new combined authorities agreed for major parts of the country and to be implemented in 2017, will the loss of this principle in the EU reduce the potential impact of this devolving policy? There are some signs that while the OECD is still promoting this case that progress might be slowed. The relationships between the devolved nations and Whitehall following the referendum have already demonstrated the lack of engagement that the centre has with its devolved governments. Moreover, there is evidence that Whitehall is attempting to take back some of the power that it has already devolved to nations. However, the devolution to English cities and sub-regions will have a far greater impact on the size and control of Whitehall than was the case in the devolved nations where there were already separate offices of state prior to devolution.

The process of devolving powers to English sub-regions began in 2007 and has been a policy across three governments – Labour, the Conservative–Liberal Democrat coalition and the Conservative government. This longstanding commitment has not been matched with open and clear policy statements of intent but rather a mix and match approach to achieve different devolved 'deals' between localities and central government. These deals can be considered as a menu with

---

[2]   UN (2016) 'The New Urban Agenda', https://habitat3.org/the-new-urban-agenda

most items on offer to most localities and an expectation that although all may not be available at the outset they will gradually be filled in. Although the Mayor of London has operated devolved powers over expenditure since 1999 the newly elected Mayor of Greater Manchester will have greater powers over issues such as health and social care. Where new powers are provided to the new directly elected mayors who will be in post following 2017 elections, such as the provision of housing and creating a strategic plan, these will be available to all and where London does not have these powers there is an expectation that they will be backfilled.

While it may be argued that during the period of Brexit negotiation that Whitehall will be too busy to consider further English devolution it may also be the case that as the civil service will be responsible for the policy areas that are likely to be back in the UK's domain following Brexit then it may be less concerned that powers are lost through increasingly devolved government in the English sub-regions.

The progress in devolution below nation level has also been an issue in Scotland, Wales and Northern Ireland. In the latter, the review of public administration has led to the implementation of new local authorities with wider and more strategic powers from 2016 onwards. These may not be sub-regional in scope but are larger than existed before and are moving in this direction. In Wales, there have been a number of attempts to encourage local authorities to work together in larger strategic units that represent functional economic areas but these have failed so far and the Welsh government is currently looking at voluntary cooperation on the English model that preceded combined authorities. In Scotland, there has also been some discussion about local government reorganisation. In 2006, four major strategic planning areas were designed for the Functional Economic Areas of Edinburgh, Glasgow, Dundee and Aberdeen but in 2015 the Scottish government announced that it would be reviewing these although without much indication of whether a similarly strategic form of governance would be implemented across the whole of Scotland.

However, there is some evidence that the UK government has been encouraging the sub-regional economic model in Scotland, Wales and

Northern Ireland through the award of city deals. These contractual forms of agreement between the state and the locality take the form of territorial pacts that have been used to implement Europe 2020, the EU's macroeconomic programme to deal with the economic crisis of 2007 and that has been in operation from 2010. This programme and hence the city deals will come to an end in 2020 and this will coincide with the likely date of Brexit. However, these city deals have provided a means to nudge FEAs into cooperative working arrangements in exchange for specific additional funding to be spent within their areas and potentially more freedoms. These city deals started in England and their extension to the other nations raises interesting questions not least as all of the issues within the deals are already devolved. In this case why is there a need for Whitehall to get involved? The first answer to this question may be the need of the UK government to deliver on some key aspects of Europe 2020 through these preferred forms of territorial pacts. There may also be some willingness of the governments of the nations to accept this intervention as both a means of bringing in additional funding but also as a mechanism to encourage new governance forms in their nations which are otherwise politically difficult to raise or implement. Finally, there has also been some reluctance by the national governments to devolve further, with an assumption that their scale is sufficiently local.

The contractual form of devolution through city deals may be used post Brexit as they provide a different mechanism for change. These vertical contracts across the state are different from the horizontal contracts between localities that are the next stage in re-fashioning the local governance institutions. The horizontal and vertical measures can work together over longer periods of time.

There are strong internal and external arguments for the continuation of these policies for devolution. While Whitehall civil servants were less keen on devolution than the government, the advent of Brexit with its potential promise of repatriating policies that provide more work and power for Whitehall may offset any slowing down of this policy; the scale of progress towards new combined authorities and directly elected mayors in England may also have passed a tipping point that will see this process continue for the foreseeable future although local governance arrangements within the UK are notoriously durable over the medium term. Future reform of the House of Lords could tie directly elected seats or representatives to these new sub-regions although this seems like a longer-term possibility. Also, if the UK does not leave the EU for any reason, will there be an attempt to reverse devolution so that the civil service will again be able to control the purse strings and policy agenda, or will it attempt to transfer itself into the new larger authorities and exert influence through the day to day management of these devolved activities?

Implications for climate change and the environment

The EU's programme for the environment has been strong since 1972 when the first Scandinavian countries became member states and it has been integrated into the single market as part of the determination of specific projects and investment as well as providing regulations for all manufactured goods. The EU strengthened its environment programme in anticipation of the UN Earth summit in 1992 and since then has been an active participant in UN environment summits and was a signatory for all member states of the Paris climate change agreement that came into effect on 4 November 2016. Following Brexit, the UK will remain as a signatory of this Paris climate change convention and will need to demonstrate how it is abiding by its international agreements.

At the same time, the EU will progress its own legislation to ensure that the UN convention is implemented in ways that complement and support the single market and wider objectives across the EU. The extent to which the UK will be part of the discussion of these legal measures will depend on the nature of its longer-term relationship. However, if any companies wish to undertake trade with those in the EU they will need to comply with any environmental legislation agreed through regulations and directives. Although this will be in effect on a case by case basis for individual trades, the UK government may find that it is more efficient to adopt the same legislation as the rest of the

EU in order to be able to gain maximum economies. Without this UK companies may have to meet UN compliance legislation in the UK and EU which may differ at the margin and such compliance may add to the costs of goods and services being sold into the EU and EEA. Notwithstanding these continued UN obligations, the Environmental Audit Parliamentary Select Committee has identified the need for a new Environment Act to secure UK implementation.[3]

Implications for trade and competition

The UK's membership of the WTO binds it into agreements on trade for agriculture goods and services in the public and private sectors. Although the UK is an individual member of the WTO, the EU has taken a lead in negotiation and making WTO agreements. Each of the WTO agreements differs although they have some common features that apply to each sector. In agriculture, for example, there can be no subsidies to farmers or landowners unless specifically negotiated and agreed between the EU and WTO. In public services, competition has to be demonstrably open to all qualified private sector companies and open tendering systems such as that operated through the EU, where contracts are advertised through OJEU – the Official Journal of the European Union – and specific forms of tendering processes are required. It is also not possible for governments to provide any form of state aid to companies unless it has been explicitly agreed.

It is important to consider what will be the arrangements for the UK outside the EU. The area that is likely to be most affected following any Brexit will be agriculture. The WTO agreement on agriculture, food and agricultural products including biomass requires that specific tariffs are applied on traded goods. However, the EC's special arrangements for financial support for agriculture that assist those in rural areas and upland land management will be lost on Brexit and the UK will not

[3] www.parliament.uk/business/committees/committees-a-z/commons-select/environmental-audit-committee/news-parliament-2015/natural-environment-after-eu-report-published-16-17/

be able to provide any assistance in these sectors unless it is able to negotiate a specific arrangement with the WTO. Farmers in the UK will lose the land management subsidies that they have been receiving. This may mean that the farmers have to manage their land differently in order to remain economically viable. This may lead to more upland areas being deserted and changes in crop type and habitat management. There will also be no support provided to rural areas from the EU through these agricultural programmes. These programmes have supported those living in rural areas in broadband provision, services, tourism, river catchment management, and education and skills.

The second area that is likely to be unaffected is the process of opening up the purchase of goods and services in the public sector to the widest market. In the EU, this is frequently referred to as the OJEU process where contracts above specific levels have to be advertised in the Official Journal of the European Union so that any company in any part of the EU can tender for the work. The EU system is managed through specific legislation and compliance is reported back to the WTO. Where member states may attempt to give specific sectors, location or companies particular support through payments or reduced prices, the EU has powers to investigate these as an application of state aid and these cases can be escalated to the European Court of Justice and the member state fined. The programme for opening up public services to competition in EU member states depends on each member state; the order in which they are exposing their public services to competition may vary depending on the starting point of the volume of public services already available to competition and also the extent to which specific sectors are open or closed to competition.

A key issue within the UK in the application of OJEU processes is that the government did not appropriately implement the OJEU procedure properly at the outset. The Thatcher government was keen to support lowest price options for tenders and mistransposed the EU legislation accordingly. This meant that wider methods of setting and assessing tenders based on conditions of work, training and local supply were omitted from the processes in the UK. Public services were excluded from tendering to run other services in the

UK although this was provided for in the terms of the EU legislation. This may have reflected the extent of competition in UK public services at the outset of this process.[4] Eventually the government had to concede, with the acceptance of regulations on the transfer of staff in undertakings that were transferred from the public to the private sector, safeguarding working rights and pensions (TUPE), and the wider forms of tender specification and assessment. Although the full range of tender processes have been used in local government, central government has primarily chosen to tender on a price basis and has lost a number of tenders to overseas companies. There is some evidence that this choice of method is now changing to be more in line with the practices of other EU member states.

Once out of the EU, the UK will need to demonstrate compliance to the WTO treaties if it is not part of the single market. It will also be responsible for demonstrating that it is not engaging in state aid activities. In this case a new state aid process will need to be developed and implemented. Suppliers complain that the OJEU process is long and costly and would welcome a reduced or streamlined process post Brexit. However, there will be considerations included in replacing the EU process to demonstrate that public sector services are open for competition in a post-Brexit world and this issue seems less understood than others.

Implications for energy security

The issue of energy security is increasing in the UK not least because there are potential reductions and difficulties in obtaining oil and gas from the North Sea. In the event of Brexit, the UK will need to negotiate membership of the group that provides access to the EU energy grid and there will need to be a greater focus on local energy production. In Germany, Denmark and the Netherlands there has been such a successful commitment to the use of waste to generate energy that the reduced levels of recycling material available in these countries

[4]   Morphet, J. (2008) *Modern local government*, London: Sage.

has meant that they are purchasing landfill waste from the UK in order to keep their incinerators operational. Denmark also produces more than its total energy requirements for a year through the use of wind power. Another key issue for the UK will be the adoption of greater retrofitting technologies for domestic and commercial buildings to reduce energy consumption; these approaches have been successful in other EU member states and have never been seriously applied in the UK. If energy security is an issue then this may be an important new programme.

Finally, energy security may be enhanced through third party states that may well be willing to provide energy to the UK. The arrangements with China over its funding of Hinkley Point and potentially other nuclear power stations in Bradwell in Essex may be a major opportunity for inward investment. The role of EDF as a main suppler for Hinkley Point will maintain a link through a company based within the EU but the future relationship may not be managed under any EU–China trade agreements. Also the differences between the UK and EDF as being inside and outside the EU may cause specific difficulties as yet to be determined. There may be consequent issues as the UK has also indicated that it wishes to leave EURATOM.[5]

Security and defence policy

The existing arrangements between the UK and the EU on security and defence appear likely to remain whatever form of new relationship is agreed. It has also been argued that coming to early arrangements on these issues could oil the wheels for some of the wider issues.[6] These talks would also involve more government departments than those leading on Brexit negotiations. The existing security arrangements relate to exchanges of intelligence across borders for issues such as

[5] www.gov.uk/government/news/opening-statement-on-second-reading-of-eu-notification-of-withdrawal-bill

[6] Wintour, P. (2016) 'Defence cooperation talks with EU could delay Brexit process', *Guardian*, 18 November, www.theguardian.com/politics/2016/nov/18/defence-cooperation-talks-with-eu-could-delay-brexit-process

terrorism, organised crime, people smuggling and financial fraud including money laundering. It is also said that the Prime Minister adopted her remain position in the UK referendum based on security rather than economic arguments.

As defence is an area of policy not yet included within EU treaties, solutions for continuing or additional cooperation between the UK and the EU will be easier to achieve outside the Article 50 negotiations. On defence, the seeming reluctance of President Trump to give continuing support to NATO suggests that those in the EU who have wanted to establish an EU standing army and centre for defence will wish to move ahead. Indeed, inside the EU, it is the UK that has been arguing against this on the basis of the role of NATO. However, if the UK leaves the EU, then there are likely to be moves forward on defence issues and as the largest military force in Europe, the UK will want to maintain cooperation.

On foreign policy, the EU has been holding informal discussions between diplomats since the 1970s and this working arrangement has now developed into regular meetings between staff and also foreign ministers who meet monthly. There are also working arrangements between member state diplomats around the world who meet and discuss their positions before entering meetings or negotiations and this provides an opportunity for both greater coordination but also for the exercise of greater power within these fora. The EU appointed a High Representative for Foreign and Security Affairs for the first time in 2007 and this post was filled by the UK Commissioner Catherine Ashton. Although this role is newly developing, it was acknowledged in the review of the balance of competences undertaken by the UK government in 2013 that the EU's foreign policy role has been unsung but effective and it concluded that it would be in the UK's interest to maintain ties and work with and through this approach post Brexit.[7]

In the past, UK foreign policy has been led by international trade and a focus on securing trading relationships and agreements. This may

[7]   Dijkstra, H. (2016) 'UK and EU Foreign Policy Cooperation after Brexit', *Newsbrief*, RUSI, 5 September, https://rusi.org/publication/newsbrief/uk-and-eu-foreign-policy-cooperation-after-brexit

need to be reconsidered in a different world where trading partners are now economically stronger and where the UK no longer has the ability to determine trading rules and relationships. The world has also moved to larger trading blocks such as the EU and NAFTA, although the latter may be called into question following the election of Trump in the US. If the UK has to reset its own foreign policy, what will this be in the changing world? Will this mercantilist past be adequate?[8] Will it be focused and dependent on the Anglosphere?[9]

If the UK wants more independence to determine its foreign relationships in trade and defence, it will need to take more responsibility for negotiating and implementing them. This suggests an increase in staff and the development of more skills that suit the changing world where former rules of engagement between politicians, people and states seem to be moving. Post Brexit, the UK retains its role on the UN Security Council, in the G7, the G20 and NATO. The government has also committed to increasing defence expenditure as a fixed percentage of GDP until 2020. In terms of the exercise of soft power, the UK has English as a common language, together with common legal systems in other parts of the world. The ties through the Commonwealth are important and more focus may be expected here, although Commonwealth countries are also seeking trade agreements with the EU such as the Canadian trade agreement (CETA). The UK has also committed a fixed percentage of its GDP to be spent on international aid and this is being reviewed in terms of its reach and effectiveness.

On leaving the EU, the UK will still have defence and security relationships with member states and may further develop those with the eastern group of members. As the UK was one of the most supportive of the accession states joining the EU, there is some political

---

[8] Hughes, K. (2016) 'UK gives up foreign policy role and influence, post-Brexit', openDemocracy, 1 November, www.opendemocracy.net/can-europe-make-it/kirsty-hughes/uk-gives-up-foreign-policy-role-and-influence-post-brexit

[9] http://blogs.lse.ac.uk/brexit/2016/07/26/after-the-brexit-vote-a-formalised-anglosphere-alliance-remains-unlikely/

and diplomatic capital already in place. This group of countries is now emerging with its own agenda and operating as a more coherent unit inside the EU to counterbalance the Franco–German axis. There will also be a reduction of the EU budget after Brexit which may mean that these eastern European states may have lower levels of EU financial support in the future. The Policy Exchange has suggested that the UK's international aid might be directed towards them in these circumstances in order to maintain good working relationships. This would also ensure that the UK's departure does not generate ill will towards the UK.[10] This view was offered prior to Trump's election and stated position on closer working relations with Russia and less support for NATO. This area of engagement may become increasingly important in any event.

There have also been criticisms about the UK's lack of serious thought about its foreign policy post Brexit.[11] The Prime Minister's visit to India in November 2016 did not appear to make the progress that was expected[12] particularly in improved relations on the role of visas for Indian citizens and students, whose position in the future appears to remain unchanged. The relationship with the US is also in a more precarious position following Trump's election with his manifesto of America First. His future foreign policy is likely to be hawkish and, while it is settling into an established position, the UK has offered an early state visit for the President to meet the Queen. This could coincide with the opening of the new US Embassy in London. Trump has also suggested that it might be possible to undertake an

[10] Bew, J. and Elefteriu, G. (2016) 'Making Sense of British Foreign Policy After Brexit: some early thoughts', Britain in the World project, Policy Exchange, July, https://policyexchange.org.uk/wp-content/uploads/2016/09/british-foreign-policy-after-brexit-policy-exchange-briefing-july-2016.pdf

[11] *New Statesman* (2016) 'There is a gaping hole where Britain's foreign policy should be', www.newstatesman.com/politics/staggers/2016/11/there-gaping-hole-where-britains-foreign-policy-should-be

[12] Sud, N. (2016) 'Indians aren't impressed with Theresa May's business offer', LSE Brexit blog, 10 November, http://blogs.lse.ac.uk/brexit/2016/11/10/indians-arent-impressed-with-theresa-mays-business-offer/

early trade deal with the UK although, within WTO treaty rules, this would only formally be an option after the UK has left the EU. The UK's international trade department minister Liam Fox is also said to have the closest relationships with Trump's allies in the Republican Party than any other government member.

While the UK will still retain an independent foreign policy, it may also have to consider the costs and benefits of an isolationist position. It will also need to consider the effect its departure will have on the way in which the EU responds to its own defence agenda. The potential for changing political leadership in the member states may also have implications for the future of the EU and these remain unknown. Within the international sphere, the French will have an increasing role in organisations such as the UN, where France has already taken a lead on the climate change convention agreed in Paris in 2015. In the future, the UK may still be able to broker working arrangements with the EU that could include attendance of the Foreign Minister at the Foreign Affairs Council that meets monthly and through diplomatic negotiation around the world. The UK could also be party to statements and positions that the EU presents on issues and in response to situations that are occurring.

SIX

Beyond Brexit, what will be lost?

Introduction

Any assessment of what will be lost when the UK leaves the EU is difficult to make. This is primarily because there is no indication of the terms that will be offered when Article 50 is invoked. Although ruled out by the Prime Minister, resulting arrangements could still retain much of the existing relationship on trade, including in the single market, customs union and through the free trade area. This continuing trade relationship was the one offered by the Brexit campaigners in the run up to the referendum and appears still to be favoured by the majority of those who voted for Brexit. However, there are a number of hard line Brexit campaigners who have shifted their positions following the referendum and are now seeking for the UK to withdraw from all relationships with the EU.[1] The Prime Minister seems to have joined them in this position.

---

[1] Riley-Smith, B. and Yorke, H. (2016) 'Heavyweight Brexiteers among 60 Tory MPs to demand clean break from the EU', *Telegraph*, 19 November, www.telegraph.co.uk/news/2016/11/19/heavyweight-brexiteers-go-public-as-60-tory-mps-demand-clean-bre/

This pressure for immediate withdrawal appeared in a letter to a Sunday newspaper in November 2016 and may be in anticipation of the government's appeal to the Supreme Court regarding the High Court decision on Parliament's involvement in triggering Article 50. While the Supreme Court agreed that the governments of Scotland and Wales could be heard, they did not find in their favour. However, the Scottish Parliament will still be given a vote on repealing UK law and use the legislative consent procedure.[2]

On the side of the EU, negotiating positions may change. There has been speculation that the election of Trump may have some considerable and unanticipated influence over the view of the EU's member states and the issue of the UK's withdrawal.[3] After the French and German elections, the UK may be offered some new arrangements that would limit the free movement of labour in some way, which appears to remain the key issue for many of those who voted to leave. Any assessment of the variation between the options for trade is uncertain and organisations such as the CBI and the City of London are asking for some clarity on which line is to be pursued to provide some stability to business operation and investment.

However, in this chapter, there is an assumption that the UK will leave the EU and the discussion is focused on what will be lost in any or all of the options under consideration. It will also lean towards an examination of these losses through a hard Brexit lens in order to consider the extent of changes that will follow. There is also some discussion about the UK and EU agreeing a transitional period of potentially up to ten years in order to ensure that all the arrangements for departure are agreed in an orderly way. This long period of transition might also be destabilising and would leave open many questions of legal determination and dispute resolution. Moreover, any

[2]   https://stv.tv/news/politics/1379124-brexit-holyrood-to-have-consent-vote-on-repealing-eu-law/

[3]   European Parliament Think Tank (2016) 'The coming Trump presidency [what think tanks are thinking]', 18 November, www.europarl.europa.eu/thinktank/en/document.html?reference=EPRS_BRI(2016)589764

delays in agreements may deter investors unwilling to risk uncertainty. These transitional arrangements, as well as other potential approaches along a continuum, are yet to be agreed. The various models for these arrangements are discussed in Chapter Three. There will also be potential policies, legislation and programmes that the EU will progress after the UK leaves the EU. Again this chapter assumes that these will be beyond the UK's reach unless specific relationships are negotiated and agreed and these are set out in Chapter Seven.

In some areas of policy, the loss will be immediate if there is no transitional period including trade relationships within and between member states and also the EU negotiated trade deals with 52 countries elsewhere in the world. Other immediate losses will include access to project funding from the European Investment Bank and cohesion funding that includes access to Horizon 2020, R&D funding and support programmes used by the UK's universities and research bodies. The EU treaties that form a platform for all EU legislation will also be lost. Although EU legislation may be transposed into UK law as a necessary interim measure following on from the invoking of Article 50, every piece of EU law is tied to a specific section in the foundational treaties. If the UK transposes EU law without this anchor, how will legal disputes over the interpretation of the law be assessed? Will they need to go to the European Court of Justice or will they be determined here in the UK without these principles being part of UK law?

Other areas where there may be losses include access to the EU's foreign policies through both formal engagement in process and the informal arrangements that exist across all EU member state diplomats globally. This could exclude the UK from briefings and common positions, and reduce the UK's strengths and power around the negotiating table. This may apply to trade negotiations as well as other diplomatic issues.

The result of the UK's referendum to leave the EU has already started to have a range of impacts and influence changes in the UK, the EU and the wider international organisational community. Some of these changes have been easy to see, such as the decrease in the value of the pound and associated increases in the prices of imported goods. These changes will also bring uncertainty to future order books and the UK government has provided reassurances to the Nissan car company that it will in some way prevent or ameliorate any potential difficulties that may be caused through tariff imposition following the UK's exit from the single market, customs union or free trade area. This has caused its own problems as reassurances may now be sought by other parts of the motor industry including suppliers and any other sectors of the industry and financial services in the UK. Jaguar Land Rover has indicated that it is willing to expand in the UK subject to promises of support for energy and infrastructure from the UK government. The press reports of these reassurances have also meant that the EC is examining to see whether they constitute state aid or specific preferences that are not permitted within the EU single market. Although there may be a view that this is a short-term issue to be ignored once the UK leaves the EU, these state aid rules will apply in any kind of trade deal that the UK has with the EU and failing this they will be upheld also by the WTO. This is illustrated by the recent ruling by the WTO against the US in its tax breaks given to Boeing.[4]

The UK leaving the EU will also have effects on the union's internal operation and balance. Some of these effects are on the member states particularly those where there are growing popularist movements against the EU including in Italy, France, the Netherlands and Germany, which all have elections and referenda within a 12-month period. The governments of these countries are concerned that their longstanding commitment to the EU will be undermined and their mandate will be weakened through a rise in anti-EU parties within their legislatures.

Other countries are also considering the implications of these changes. The most affected is Ireland, which has always had a close relationship with the UK and has the most integrated trade links. The future of Ireland is now not so bound up with the UK since it joined

---

[4] BBC News (2016) 'Boeing tax break ruled unlawful by WTO', 28 November, www.bbc.co.uk/news/business-38131617

the EU and the Eurozone but the physical barrier that the UK will place between Ireland and the rest of the EU is also a barrier to easy working relationships. In this case the UK might operate more like Switzerland, which has managed to obtain EU funding for transport to ensure that the movement of goods and people in the EU will not be delayed by the need to cross Switzerland on a daily basis. The Swiss also exact road tolls in addition to the support funding they receive from the EU and receive the largest EU payments of any non-member state.

In the north of Europe, including the Netherlands and Scandinavia, the UK has been seen as an ally for liberalisation and reform. There have been good working relationships between the governments of the UK, the Netherlands and Sweden for example, but these have also been frustrated by the referendum and the continuing attitude of the UK to the EU. While these northern European countries have been supportive of the UK, if the future of the EU is without the UK then they will make other alliances with regret. To the east of Europe, Poland has been a friend of the UK since the Second World War with Polish people now living throughout the UK. These links bring skills and populations to growing and declining areas and also provide considerable financial remittances to support families at home. This migration has also created some scarcity in Poland for skilled craftsman which is being filled by Albanian in-migrants. The Polish Prime Minister has promised to be helpful to the UK although she has pointed out that the UK will need to be more flexible in its approach if it wishes to retain a positive relationship with the other member states. Poland is also part of the Visegrad group, which also includes Hungary, Slovakia and the Czech Republic. The departure of the UK could make the group's position more critical and it may expect more bargains to stay on side in a period of destabilisation.

The loss of faith in the EU by the UK is a considerable dent in its role as a major global player. For the EU, this notion of a global role and having the largest market is still a major force and the primary objective of trade deals with other blocks including the US, Canada and Australia. The UK's exit from the EU may also have other economic impacts. The German Council of Economic Advisers has pressed the German Chancellor to seek to reverse the UK's decision as they regard it as an existential economic risk.[5] Pressure on the EU leaders about being more flexible towards the UK have also come from the IMF, the OECD and the US. These economic arguments are strongly understood in the UK where there could be the loss of financial services and other companies that have located in the UK as a part of their inward investment strategies. However, as Jonathan Hill, the UK's EU commissioner until the referendum, remarked that the EU is an emotional rather than an economic project for Europe, unlike for the UK. In these circumstances, if the EU considers that it is in its best interests to maintain the UK as part of the place of Europe, it may act against its own economic interests in order to find a way to maintain the UK's membership.

These discussions are some way off and may not emerge until after the French and German elections. While the Prime Minister has stated her views on achieving hard Brexit and her globalist vision for the UK, it is yet to be seen whether this can be delivered. While the arguments of what might follow Brexit were made in the referendum campaign, this was also more of an emotional than a rational consideration, with debate with experts being sidelined through media campaigns and rhetoric. In November 2016 a complaint was made to the Crown Prosecution Service that the public were deliberately told untruths during the referendum campaign and that this should be considered as some kind of fraud.

All of these are important and they also imply that there is a need for the EU to consider its own operation and institutions. It can no longer rely on the necessity and sentiment of the post-war era and it has to make a new case to its citizens for its role. In a period of post neo-liberalism, the role of the EU in promoting social and environmental goods is well established but it has to contend with the rise of populism and individualism that is its legacy. While the EU is

[5] Henley, J. (2016) 'Prevent Brexit or face political fallout, German economists warn EU', *Guardian*, 2 November, www.theguardian.com/politics/2016/nov/02/prevent-brexit-or-face-political-fallout-german-economists-warn-eu

maintaining a steady position in relation to the UK during the Brexit process, it will also be looking to new initiatives and policies that mean more to the lives of people in Europe rather than being considered as a distant bureaucracy. This may involve giving the European Parliament greater powers so that there are clearer links between the electorate and decision making. There may also be a focus on the UN's New Urban Agenda that will enable the EU to work more closely with cities and communities through the EU's covenant of mayors. This relationship will use the EC's powers to enable it to engage directly in promoting delivery programmes that can support economic, social and territorial cohesion. Climate change targets will primarily be met through cities and urban areas and these will also be brought into these programmes.

So while the Brexit discussions are the outward sign of activity within the EU, the programme for the next budget period 2021–27 is being developed.[6] The increase in investment funds and programmes established by Juncker when he came to office in 2014 are set to increase. In the UK referendum, many areas in receipt of EU investment and support funds including Wales were advised that leaving the EU would not affect their EU funding,[7] although it was always clearly the case. Cornwall and the north east of England voted to leave but such was the lack of understanding about the implications of the referendum in these areas that, immediately following the result, local political leaders wrote to the EU to request guarantees that their funding would be maintained for the future and beyond Brexit.[8] In all options other than remain, the scale of EU funding in the UK will drop

[6] European Commission (2016) 'Investment Challenges in Energy, Transport & Digital Markets: A Forward Looking Perspective', Institutional paper 041, November, http://ec.europa.eu/economy_finance/publications/eeip/pdf/ip041_en.pdf

[7] BBC News (2016) 'Welsh EU cash 'maintained' after Brexit, say vote Leave', 14 June, www.bbc.co.uk/news/uk-wales-politics-36523232

[8] Worley, W. (2016) 'Cornwall issues plea to keep EU funding after voting for Brexit', Independent, 24 June, www.independent.co.uk/news/uk/home-news/brexit-cornwall-issues-plea-for-funding-protection-after-county-overwhelmingly-votes-in-favour-of-a7101311.html; Hailstone, J. (2016)

either to much lower levels as might be achieved through a Norway or EGTC model or very rapidly to zero unless through specifically negotiated individual projects and schemes.

Universities: loss of students, staff, funding and cooperation

UK universities will suffer at least two major losses following Brexit.[9] The first is through the number of European students and academic staff attracted to the UK and the second is through research funding and networks between academics. There will also be specific effects on science research. Overall UK universities contribute to the economy as well as to business innovation.

All universities within the EU are harmonising qualifications through the Bologna process,[10] which will be lost unless specifically included as part of the Article 50 negotiations. In 2013–14, there were 125,300 EU students studying at UK universities compared with approximately 15,000 UK students studying full time at EU universities outside the UK plus 15,000 UK students spending time in the other EU countries as part of EU ERASMUS programmes. At present those students already studying in the UK and those who enter UK universities in 2017 are guaranteed to be able to remain students in the UK on the same basis as before the referendum. This means that there will be no changes in their loans status or fee eligibility. Further EU students will pay the same fees as home students for their whole course even if it finishes after the UK has left the EU. After this, EU students will be expected to pay the same fees as overseas students. The ERASMUS

'Council leaders issue Brexit warnings', theMJ.co.uk, 24 June, www.themj. co.uk/Council-leaders-issue-Brexit-warnings/204537

[9] House of Commons Library (2016) 'Effect of exiting the EU on higher education', 21 November, http://researchbriefings.parliament.uk/ ResearchBriefing/Summary/CDP-2016-0224#fullreport

[10] European Commission, Education and Training, 'The Bologna Process and the European Higher Education Area', http://ec.europa.eu/education/policy/ higher-education/bologna-process_en

programme arrangements will remain until the UK leaves the EU and will subsequently be lost.

Universities receive research funding from a range of different EU programmes. Some funds are made available via the cohesion funds that are channelled through European Structural Investment Funds (ESIF) via local authorities and LEPs (local enterprise partnerships). Universities will receive about €1.6 billion between 2014 and 2020 from these funds, that will be guaranteed by the government until the UK leaves the EU, after which cohesion funds will not be available except for specific projects negotiated through countries remaining within the EU. The current cohesion funds programme is in place until 2020 and it is uncertain what will happen beyond this. If the Brexit negotiating period extends into the next EU budget for the period 2021–27, the UK's position on cohesion funding will need to be considered. While the UK remains a member of the EU then it is eligible to receive funding. Decisions on this funding will need to be made in the next EU budget round that will be concluded in 2020. A second major source of EU funding for university research is through Horizon 2020 and UK universities were expected to receive £2 billion in the first two years of the Horizon 2020 programme 2014–20. In both cases the government has guaranteed project funding even where they might end beyond the UK's exit from the EU. While the UK contributes between 11–12% of the EU's budget each year, it is estimated that UK universities receive approximately 15% of EU research funding. On 21 November 2016, the Prime Minister guaranteed £2 billion a year for research and development from 2020 onwards although these funds will not necessarily all be received by UK universities and may be available for business.

This funding also attracts leading research talent from across the world to the UK. Much of the research work has a direct impact on business and innovation within the UK as well as elsewhere in the EU. The uncertainty about the UK's future in the EU means that some academics and departments are already being sidelined or excluded from research bids being submitted to the EU as academics in other member states are associating UK membership of a bid team with risk and potential failure of the application. During the referendum campaign, leave supporters said that there would be more funding for UK university research funding[11] although there has as yet been no subsequent discussion of this. In the meantime, universities are seeking to strengthen their global links in order to reassure potential researchers who might want to join them and also to meet new funding bodies. Some universities are also considering establishing branches within the EU and taking the same route as business.[12]

A future issue to consider will be the position of EU staff who work in British universities. Although there are no current plans to introduce specific visa arrangements or quotas, in the longer term their position is uncertain. This may have a considerable effect on university staff seeking posts elsewhere within the EU and EU staff no longer seeking to work in the UK. Some universities have employed legal expertise specifically to support their EU staff and ensure that any necessary legal processes are undertaken to assist them in maintaining their posts.

The UK Parliament's Education Select Committee has established an inquiry into the effects of Brexit on universities teaching and students and has been receiving evidence. The effect on universities in terms of research funding will be considered by the Parliamentary Select Committee on Business Energy and Industrial Strategy. The potential losses to UK universities of students, staff and research funding/activities following Brexit are considerable and will not be capable of being maintained to the same levels under any model other than remain.

[11] Goodfellow, J. (2016) 'Brexit: What will it mean for universities, students and academics?', *Telegraph*, 1 July, www.telegraph.co.uk/education/2016/07/01/brexit-what-will-it-mean-for-universities-students-and-academics

[12] BBC News (2016) 'Brexit: UK universities consider EU branches', 23 September, www.bbc.co.uk/news/education-37451392

Addressing inequalities: health, poverty and skills

Through its foundational treaties,[13] the EU has had a core commitment to addressing social and economic inequality, which is one of the measures that it uses to design, implement and fund policy. As a result of Brexit, the UK will lose this fundamental principle in its own activities and this will need to be considered as a loss. This approach to equality and redistribution may be further undermined. Not only will the UK lose the core principle of addressing inequality, but it may also be that any appeal to these principles is not properly heard[14] due to popularist and nationalistic sentiment emerging in political discourse.

In terms of health, member states have the leading role in the provision of health care, although the EU has major roles in some aspects of health policy and delivery,[15] including the application of standards of equity for access and treatment. The areas of primary and secondary health care where the EU is involved include the European health insurance card (EHIC) that allows EU citizens to receive health care on the same basis as nationals anywhere in the EU. This will be lost to UK citizens if not specifically negotiated as part of the single market post Brexit. The EU has a role in overseeing the competition for providers of health care through the single market and the application of WTO competiton rules. The EU also has a major role in the standards used for medical products and drugs. In the UK, the EU health programme is promoted and delivered by the NHS.[16]

The EU has a greater role in public health where many of its policies and legislation have a direct bearing on prevention. This also includes

---

[13] Treaty of Rome 1957; Treaty for the European Union – Maastricht 1992; Treaty of Lisbon 2007.

[14] Ash, T.G. (2016) 'Populists are out to divide us. They must be stopped', *Guardian*, 11 November, www.theguardian.com/commentisfree/2016/nov/11/populists-us

[15] EUROPA, 'Health', https://europa.eu/european-union/topics/health_en

[16] NHS European Office (2016) 'EU Health Programme 2014–2020', 2 November, www.nhsconfed.org/regions-and-eu/nhs-european-office/accessing-eu-funding/eu-health-programme-2014-2020

a focus on specific groups such as children and older people. The application of subsidiarity to public health programmes for prevention have been determined as being the responsibility of local authorities and much of the EU legal and policy framework operates at this level once implemented through regulations. This includes obesity, immunisation, air quality, pollutants in water supplies, chemical use for bio-management, transport accidents, patient safety and public health control of epidemics. It promotes the role of open spaces and recreation for mental health issues. In the EU, social care is defined as a right. It also includes issues such as health technology and the provision of e-health and digital services. It is also concerned with the safety and security of personal health data and patient records.

Many of the staff who work in the NHS and social care in the UK are from the EU.[17] Any change in the work requirements for EU nationals after Brexit may have a significant impact on these services; there are already staff shortages that cannot be filled. The King's Fund has argued that it is a central issue when considering any future negotiations on the free movement of workers between the EU and the UK, including a clear and early statement about the ongoing rights of those already here.

On Brexit, some of these health care matters will remain as they are included in other wider UK agreements through the WTO for health care provision and through the UN and World Health Organization (WHO) for public health. However, the EHIC, together with the drive for a more coordinated and devolved approach in health, will be lost unless specifically addressed in the negotiations. There will also be concerns about the position of EU staff in the UK providing health services and social care who may be lost directly or who may decide not to take a job in the UK in the first place on an assessment of future career risks.

---

[17] House of Lords Library (2016) 'Leaving the European Union: NHS and Social Care Workforce', 18 November, http://researchbriefings.parliament. uk/ResearchBriefing/Summary/LLN-2016-0061#fullreport

Culture and heritage

The EU has a role in supporting culture and heritage within its area and with external countries[18] and it implements its role through the European agenda for culture agreed in 2007.[19] This has been translated into programmes that relate to other sectors of the EU's responsibilities including trade and the single market, training and skills, the digital strategy, tourism and sport. The programme supports festivals for the arts, literature and other cultural activities at national and local levels and includes the designation of cities as cultural capitals for annual periods. Like other EU programmes, the cultural strategy is delivered in agreed periods – currently Creative Europe 2014–20.[20]

The UK has had a long tradition of supporting and developing its heritage assets, digital economy and tourism so it can be argued that not all this will be lost on Brexit. However, some UK cities such as Glasgow, Liverpool and Hull have benefited from their designation as European cultural capitals and extra support from these programmes to attract visitors and undertake skills training, improvement of facilities and public pride in place.

---

[18] 'Consolidated version of the Treaty on the Functioning of the European Union', Official Journal of the European Union, C 326/47, 26 October 2012, http://eur-lex.europa.eu/legal-content/EN/TXT/PDF/?uri=CELEX:12012E/TXT&from=en#page=75&zoom=100&view=FitB

[19] Commission of the European Communities (2007) 'Communication from the Commission to the European Parliament, the Council, the European Economic and Social Committee and the Committee of the Regions on a European agenda for culture in a globalizing world', COM(2007) 242 final, 10 May, http://eur-lex.europa.eu/legal-content/EN/TXT/PDF/?uri=CELEX:52007DC0242&from=EN

[20] European Commission, Creative Europe, 'About', https://ec.europa.eu/programmes/creative-europe/about_en

Funding and trade agreements

It has been calculated that any financial benefits of the UK leaving the EU in terms of payments of £8 billion per annum will be lost if the UK's GDP slips by 0.6%[21] and current calculations estimate that the UK's GDP will be between 2% and 7% lower by 2030. These losses are to the general economy and the UK will also lose specific investment directly from the EU or funded through the European Investment Bank (EIB). In 2015, the EIB supported UK projects through loans of €7.6 billion, the largest ever engagement in the country. The EIB states that:

> For 2015, energy projects accounted for 24% of total investments, while transport and water claimed respectively 22% and 21% respectively of the 2015 figure. Another notable beneficiary has been health and education which jointly accounted for 20%. Over the past five years (2011–2015) the Bank has invested over EUR 29 billion in the British economy.[22]

Post Brexit, there is uncertainty about any future access to funding for infrastructure, although it is likely that existing loans will be honoured. There will be a loss of access to funds that have supported major infrastructure for government projects including the Jubilee Line, the second Severn Crossing and the Channel Tunnel and also provided loans for local authorities to purchase housing. Current projects include improving the Port of Liverpool and retrofitting housing to sustainable and greener standards in London, £60 million for trains in East Anglia, £82 million for the Humber offshore transmission link and £160 million for R&D in the automotive industries. The EIB has

---

[21] Mitchell, I. (2016) 'Free trade agreements and the implications of Brexit for the UK', Institute of Fiscal Studies, presentation to APPG for Social Science and Policy, 1 November, www.esrc.ac.uk/files/news-events-and-publications/evidence-briefings/presentation-by-ian-mitchell-ifs/

[22] European Investment Bank, 'The EIB in the United Kingdom', www.eib.org/projects/regions/european-union/united-kingdom/index.htm

also funded loans for major hospital development. The EIB has used some of its funding for projects outside the EU, but any continued lending to the UK post Brexit would require a unanimous vote by all member states.[23]

For project funding and EIB loans that have been allocated to the UK through the ESIF programmes delivered through LEPs and combined authorities, the government initially indicated that only those schemes that had been approved by the Autumn Statement on 23 November 2016 would be honoured but this has now been extended to all projects signed off before the UK leaves the EU.[24]

The EU has 67 trade agreements with nations around the world that will be lost once the UK leaves the EU unless these are specially retained within the agreements. If the UK stays within the single market then it will retain access to these agreements but if its final location is beyond the free trade area and customs union then it will not. Of the UK's 50 top trade areas in 2015, 10 are covered by these trade agreements. Of the other 40, 18 are EU members and 33 are where the EU has no trade agreement in force. There is no trade agreement with the US with either the UK or the EU which was the UK's largest goods export market to a single country in 2015,[25] although the EU represents the largest market overall where 40% of trade is located. While the UK may be able to negotiate a trade agreement with the US this may be smaller than initially expected as the US takes an 'America First' stance under President Trump.

In terms of other trade agreements, these will take some time to negotiate. Trade agreements are primarily for goods rather than

[23] Ayres, S. (2016) 'Brexit: future funding from the European Investment Bank?', Second Reading, 21 November, https://secondreading.uk/economy/brexit-future-funding-from-the-european-investment-bank/

[24] Clayden, S. (2016) 'Javid committed to extend pledge to match EU funding', TheMJ.co.uk, 9 November, www.themj.co.uk/Javid-committed-to-extend-pledge-to-match-EU-funding/205961

[25] House of Commons Library (2016) 'List of EU trade agreements', 21 November, http://researchbriefings.parliament.uk/ResearchBriefing/Summary/CBP-7792#fullreport

services, which would include the requirement for harmonised regulation as would be the case within the EU. It is not anticipated that new UK trade deals will be able to fully compensate for those arrangements lost within the EU.[26] The levels of trade between the UK and the BRICS (Brazil, Russia, India, China, South Africa) markets is small with China representing 3% of trade value and India 2%. In negotiating any trade agreements, the UK will also have to manage its own enforcement cases through the WTO, which has a much lower enforcement rate than the cases brought to the EU each year.[27]

Not being within the EU also means that the UK may lose investment from third countries that regard the UK as an attractive gateway into the EU. This offer was particularly prevalent during the 1980s Thatcher years but it has remained a continuing feature of UK inward investment. This is likely to affect a range of sectors including space and other hi tech industries based in the UK. Being outside the EU would require tariffs for these companies when selling their goods to the EU. There would also be tariffs on the supply chain for parts integral to the automotive industry.[28] Meanwhile, these automotive companies, like companies in many other sectors, are already receiving invitations to relocate inside other EU member states.[29]

[26] Economic and Social Research Council (2016) 'Trade options after Brexit', November, www.esrc.ac.uk/news-events-and-publications/evidence-briefings/trade-options-after-brexit

[27] Armstrong, A. (2016) 'Free trade agreements and the implications of Brexit for the UK', National Institute of Economic and Social Research, presentation to the All Party Parliamentary Group, 1 November, www.esrc.ac.uk/files/news-events-and-publications/evidence-briefings/presentation-by-angus-armstrong/

[28] Lords Select Committee (2016) 'Brexit: trade in automotives, aerospace and defence goods examined', 3 November, www.parliament.uk/business/committees/committees-a-z/lords-select/eu-external-affairs-subcommittee/news-parliament-2015/brexit-automotive-aerospace-defence/

[29] Asthana, A. and Mason, R. (2016) 'Japanese companies in UK 'already receiving offers from EU", *Guardian*, 31 October, www.theguardian.com/politics/2016/oct/31/nissan-assurances-over-brexit-cannot-be-published-says-business-secretary

Outside the EU, the UK might be able to fund this level of public and private investment through bond and loan facilities with sovereign wealth funds but these may vary in their availability depending on the world financial markets. The EIB application for loan funds is not competitive and will depend on whether the project is supporting the delivery of EU and national objectives. The EIB has been a significant provider of funds to UK local authorities for housing renovations or purchase for rent at a time when other funding has not been easily available. The UK may wish to negotiate a continuing agreement/ arrangement with the EIB post Brexit but as noted earlier this would need the approval of all other member states and the terms may not be so favourable.

Free movement

Although much of the debate in the period before the UK referendum on EU membership was concerned with the issue of free movement of workers coming to the UK from the EU, there was less consideration of the loss of free movement for UK citizens in the EU. This includes those who work, live or travel in other member states. In terms of working, any restrictions on EU nationals working in the UK can be expected to be mirrored by those imposed on the UK. This may be significant and have a considerable effect on companies who locate their staff in other EU member states. For those who live in other EU member states, this will primarily affect those who live in Spain in retirement. These UK citizens may have lived in their retirement location for many years but may no longer be entitled to live there in the future without specific permits. Similarly, those who own holiday properties in France and other countries may require special permits to own property and face restrictions on the use of the properties for business. For visiting the EU, there has already been some discussion about an EU visa system for UK citizens entering the EU that would require a payment of £5 or £10. This will also put those with UK passports outside the E-borders system that is now used for easier electronic passport control.

The issue of free movement was central to the debates held during the referendum campaign and appears to be the minimal component of any agreement between the UK and the EU. Free movement is one of the four single market freedoms and the EU members have always underlined their position on maintaining this principle. However, this position was taken when it seemed unlikely that the UK would vote to leave the EU and before the rise in popularism across the EU was boosted by Brexit and the outcome of the US presidential election. The issue of free movement of people is also high on the agenda in other states as part of the outcome of the refugee and migrant crisis and the threats issued by Turkey's President about the encouragement of refugees in camps there to enter the EU if it implements a halt on membership discussions on the basis of human rights issues as proposed by the European Parliament. There is also a claim that, unlike other member states, the UK has not used the legal powers that it has to manage freedom of movement and if it had, this would have ameliorated many of the concerns of Brexit voters.[30] The EU may make some shifts on free movement as already agreed with some of the enclave and micro states but this is not certain and at this stage it would be appropriate to consider free movement from the UK to the EU to be lost.

The use of English as an EU official language

Once the UK leaves the EU, English will be replaced as an official language. Until 1992, the EU's business was conducted in its only official language French; English then became the second official language. Post Brexit, English will be replaced by another language – with German being the most favoured candidate. In practical terms all EU documents are published in English often as a single language and this has benefits for those using legislation, policies and programmes. After Brexit, those companies and institutions still operating within the

[30] https://brexit853.wordpress.com/2016/09/27/powers-that-the-uk-has-failed-to-use-to-control-eu-freedom-of-movement-directive/

EU will face significant extra translation costs as part of doing business. It will also reduce the UK's influence in the EU and potentially the role of English in the world.

Post-political methods of policy and delivery

One major change and loss to Westminster and Whitehall will be the mechanisms that have been used to introduce new EU policy and legislation. Since the UK joined the EU in 1972, the operational practices of governments and particularly civil servants have been to both propose policy and legislation that has been agreed by the UK in the EU as domestic initiatives and then to 'gold plate'[31] them – to add more elements and components than have been agreed within the EU with other countries. In this way, the government and civil service are able to attach other policy objectives to these implementation approaches, but the EC has complained that Europe is then blamed for these additional elements and related regulatory costs.

These approaches are apparent on many policies and the examination of one day's government news will provide an example. On 29 November 2016, the Prime Minister announced a consultation on corporate governance in companies including the shareholders' role in setting executive pay which is also to be linked with performance. Commentators on radio and television were suggesting that this is a common approach recently introduced into other EU member states. What they did not say was that there was an EU decision to progress these reforms in 2012[32] and the UK like other member states

---

[31] Miller, V. (2011) *EU legislation: Government action on 'gold-plating'*, SN/1A/5943 (London: House of Commons Library) 19 April; European Parliament Directorate-General for Internal Policies (2014) '"Gold-plating" in the EAFRD: To what extent do national rules unnecessarily add to complexity and, as a result, increase the risk of errors?', www.europarl.europa.eu/RegData/etudes/etudes/join/2014/490684/IPOL-JOIN_ET(2014)490684_EN.pdf

[32] European Commission (2012) 'Action Plan: European company law and corporate governance – a modern legal framework for more engaged

is implementing them. A second example was the announcement from Ofcom that it intended to request that BT establishes a separate company for OpenReach, its broadband provider. This issue was also coming before the European Parliament at the same time.[33] The third issue is the opening of work on the A14, one of the Trans European Networks, although this was not mentioned in the news release[34] and where it is described as one of the government's schemes for road improvements and funded from central government budgets. This is typical of announcements on many days including reports of EU meetings attended by ministers in which the EU is omitted from the heading and text.

For much of UK policy and legislation that is agreed by the UK within the EU, the intellectual challenge for the civil service is to find policy lines in which it is able to dress the delivery in ways that are ideologically acceptable to ministers and do not relate to the EU. The announcement of corporate governance mentioned above provides an example where this fits into the Prime Minister's agenda of restoring the sense of the welfare state and some voice for those who remain angry about the economic crisis in 2008. The same approach was taken with Margaret Thatcher and the introduction of competition in public services, which was not mentioned in her 1979 manifesto but became a defining feature of her time in office. Following Brexit, the civil

shareholders and sustainable companies', COM(2012) 740 final, http://eur-lex.europa.eu/legal-content/EN/TXT/PDF/?uri=CELEX:52012DC0740&from=EN

[33] European Parliament Think Tank (2016) 'WIFI4EU – Promotion of internet connectivity in local communities', 28 November, www.europarl.europa.eu/thinktank/en/document.html?reference=EPRS_BRI(2016)593561; European Parliament Think Tank (2016) 'Body of European Regulators for Electronic Communications (BEREC)', 28 November, www.europarl.europa.eu/thinktank/en/document.html?reference=EPRS_BRI(2016)593560

[34] Makey, J. (2016) 'Work starts on £1.5 billion A14 upgrade', *Cambridge News*, 28 November, www.cambridge-news.co.uk/news/local-news/work-starts-15-billion-a14-12241791; European Commission Innovation and Networks Executive Agency, 'TEN-T Projects: United Kingdom', https://ec.europa.eu/inea/ten-t/ten-t-projects/projects-by-country/united-kingdom

service will need to return to developing and delivering policies from scratch. This is a different skill set from commenting and negotiating on policies and then considering how to implement them.

The agreement of UK policies within the EU has also led to an anti- or post-political approach to statecraft. Where policies have been agreed within the EU and enacted through regulations, there is no need for Parliament to approve them and frequently these policies appear with little or no provenance or justification. They have no narrative and emerge as orphans into the policy arena.[35] Following Brexit, the tools of statecraft will need to change. With no foundational treaties to underpin subsidiarity, devolution, major transport routes, redistributive policies between the nations and localities, trade and market policies, and energy and health matters, the civil service will need to be expanded to develop these roles again. There will be less confidence in developing policies as they will not have the same legal backing from the outset and there will need to be a reintroduction of white and green policy papers together with new government websites to discuss and track policy issues. At present the UK government relies on EU websites to provide this policy anchoring and legislative links. This is already being signalled through the return in the use of white and green papers to introduce policy – an approach that had been lost since 2010.

The drive and agenda for policy making will be lost as will the EU legislative implementation roles of the devolved nations. In an interesting move, the government has sought to devolve non-EU matters to the new directly elected mayors and their combined authorities in England including health. This will provide more stability for the Brexit transition. Otherwise, these mayors, like the Mayor of London, will be in the same position as the First Ministers of Scotland, Wales and Northern Ireland in having their governing basis largely removed and lost post Brexit unless it is replaced in other ways.

---

[35] Morphet, J. (2013) *How Europe shapes British public policy*, Bristol: Policy Press.

SEVEN

Beyond Brexit, what will be foregone?

Introduction

While much will change or be lost following the EU's departure from the EU, it is also important to consider what is being foregone – what future policies and programmes being developed by the EU now will the UK no longer benefit from in the future? The referendum on leaving the EU has occurred in the middle of the EU's programme cycle 2014–20. This is the period of the EU budget, and of the appointment of its main officer holders – that is the President of the European Council, the President of the European Commission and the High Representative for External Affairs. The European Parliament holds elections every five years with the next in 2019, immediately before the budget setting for the next programme. The programme period lasts for seven years to enable the programmes to span at least one general election in every member state so that each country has the potential to reset its policy and delivery agenda.

Funding for local investment

The adoption of the seven-year cycle has brought together programmes so that they can operate within the same temporal space and also allows for potential interconnections between projects. However, there is concern within the EU that the synchronicity of programme timing is not really changing the silos and gaps between them. There is also concern that the programmes, developed and supported by different directorates general, may also be cutting across each other and creating a difficult set of choices when it comes to delivery in specific places. The development of the cohesion programme, which brings together all of the sub-state policy and delivery at city and regional level from 2014 through the Common Provisions Regulation,[1] was a first attempt. This programme has at its core the development of a strategic plan that has a set of objectives and a delivery strategy that are local but which also link to the EU's economic programme for the same period. These strategic plans, or Integrated Territorial Investment[2] strategies, also have to be set to deliver the economic objectives as agreed in Europe 2020. To fit within these at a more local level – for areas of 10,000–150,000 population – the Regulation also included provision of Community Led Local Development (CLLD)[3] plans and programmes. However, the problems related to other major programmes, such as Trans European Networks, energy, environment, digital communications and some R&D, still remain in their own silos.

While the 2014–20 programme is being delivered and is the main focus of EU activity within member states, the EC is developing the programme for the next programming and budgetary cycle – that for 2021–27. This next programme may well represent the first that

[1] Regulation (EU) No 1303/2013, http://eur-lex.europa.eu/legal-content/EN/TXT/PDF/?uri=CELEX:32013R1303&:PDF

[2] European Commission (2015) 'Scenarios for Integrated Territorial Investments', 2014–20, http://ec.europa.eu/regional_policy/en/information/publications/reports/2015/scenarios-for-integrated-territorial-investments

[3] European Network for Rural Development, 'Community-led local development (CLLD)', http://enrd.ec.europa.eu/themes/clld_en

the UK has not been part of for 50 years. It is in this that further integration of EC programmes, in ways that are more targeted towards spatial and territorial considerations, will emerge. In this chapter some consideration of what is likely to be delivered in the next and subsequent cycles will be considered.

In the UK, EU funding is generally associated with two things. The first is the structural funds that areas may receive as part of cohesion programmes to reduce economic and spatial disparities between places that may be peripheral, sparsely populated or on islands (European Structural and Investment Funds, ESIF).[4] These funds are also available in some forms to FEAs for transport, environmental projects, R&D, rural areas and skills.[5] These have largely been subsumed into a narrative of central government programmes and it was only following the UK referendum on EU membership that many localities appreciated for the first time the origins of the growth funds or support for skills or transport. EU funding has also become associated with the contributions that the UK makes to the EU and while Brexit may mean a change in these, any access to any form of market with the EU will require payments to the EU so the longer-term savings may not be as high as expected. There will also be other reductions in payments to farmers for the management of their land. These subsidies are provided through a special agreement that the EU has negotiated with the WTO. When the UK leaves the EU, the UK will be prohibited from paying this subsidy by the terms of the treaties it has signed with the WTO and its preceding organisation, GATT.

In addition to these funds that are more commonly known about, the EU has provided funding for other major projects, particularly

[4] 'European Structural and Investment Funds (ESIF)', www.gov.uk/european-structural-investment-funds

[5] London Enterprise Panel, 'European Funding Strategy 2014–20', https://lep.london/publication/european-funding-strategy-2014-20; Swindon Wilstshire Local Enterprise Partnership, 'European Structural Investment Fund (ESIF)', www.swlep.co.uk/programmes/European-Structural-Investment-Fund-(ESIF); Leicester & Leicestershire Enterprise Partnership, 'ESIF', www.llep.org.uk/strategies-and-plans/esif

transport and infrastructure. For the Trans European Transport (TEN-T) projects,[6] there is a support payment of 40% for design and smaller amounts for implementation. These contributions have gone into major station refurbishments including London termini, Manchester, Leeds and Liverpool. Funding for transport has also been provided for specific schemes including HS1, the West Coast main line electrification and Crossrail.[7] EU funding has also contributed to extending public transport lines to major airports. Other beneficiaries of EU funding have been universities through research programmes such as Horizon 2020[8] and student and staff exchanges between universities.

The EU has also provided funds for public bodies for projects or to assist purchases or repairs. This is through the European Investment Bank (EIB), which provides loans at competitive rates of interest. According to Article 309 of the TFEU, the task of the EIB is to contribute to the balanced and steady development of the internal market in the interest of the Union and to support projects that seek to develop less-developed regions; to seek to modernise or convert undertakings, or develop new activities which cannot be completely financed by means available in individual member states; these projects should be of common interest to several member states. It also contributes to the promotion of economic, social and territorial cohesion. It supports the implementation of the Europe 2020 objectives. EIB activities focus on four priority areas: innovation and skills, access to finance for smaller businesses, climate action, and strategic infrastructure. It is estimated that the EIB loan book for the UK stands at €50 billion and those loans have been used to fund infrastructure, purchase housing and improve housing stock. The

---

[6] European Commission, Trans-European Transport Network, 'Welcome to our public portal', http://ec.europa.eu/transport/infrastructure/tentec/tentec-portal/site/en/abouttent.htm

[7] European Commission, 'TEN-T', http://ec.europa.eu/transport/infrastructure/tentec/tentec-portal/map/mobile.html

[8] European Commission, 'Horizon 2020', https://ec.europa.eu/programmes/horizon2020/

EIB fund has been available to local authorities as well as for central government activities. A newer fund provides investment for Europe set up by EC President Juncker in 2014 to support infrastructure. Although not much discussed, the UK has had almost the highest number of projects funded in this way, including those for infrastructure and hospitals.[9] This fund will be expanded in the next cycle 2021–27.

Once Brexit has occurred, the UK's access to these grant and loan funds will be lost or much reduced and if the government wishes to maintain the same levels of payment to support localities, people and projects it will need to find other sources of finance. This might be available through pension funds; Canadian and Australian pensions have been particularly attracted to investing in UK infrastructure in the past. The UK is also attempting to attract funding from China and sovereign wealth funds. Other funds will need to be found through the markets or it may be that programmes are stopped. Some parts of the public sector, like universities, health and local government, may be able to raise bonds for capital investment from other sources.

Transport

The EU support for transport projects through policies, legislation and funding have had a significant impact on transport investment in the UK since 1996. Before this, there was very little investment in public transport with a focus on roads and car use, particularly during the Thatcher era. However, since the agreement of the TEN-T, linking parts of the EU together, there has been significant investment in different transport modes and routes. The TEN-T require that there are three transport modes in each designated corridor. The A14 corridor, which has been part of the TEN-T from Crete to Donegal, has seen road and rail improvement including other projects, such as the guided busway in Cambridge that have been part of this corridor provision.

---

[9]   European Investment Bank (2016) 'Investment Plan for Europe – The first year', www.eib.org/infocentre/publications/all/investment-plan-for-europe. htm

Since designating these networks and corridors in 1996, the EC has been supporting their implementation and delivery. There has been some modification to the projects but once agreed these routes have not had to continually demonstrate their needs for funding and delivery of components within member states. This support has not only been the designation of the core networks across Europe and its key nodes but it has also provided the legal underpinning for these networks through regulations. These regulations have meant that member states have not been required to take these projects to their own Parliaments for agreement. In England this has primarily been achieved through the projects supported through the National Policy Statements and the 2008 Planning Act; the Act also prescribes a development consent order process that does not have to justify the principle of development, only how the scheme is to be implemented.

When the UK leaves the EU, these transport corridors, redefined in 2013, will not be applicable in the UK. This will mean that major transport routes will require primary legislation and planning appeals will have to start one stage back. Parliament may be able to hold on to these powers for a period of time as provided for in Article 50 but at some point there will need to be a replacement for the anchor given to transport routes and projects that can no longer rely on the cohesion principles within the European treaties.

There will also be issues about the comprehensive networks within the core network. In the 2013 regulations there were provisions that require the designation of a secondary or comprehensive network to determine which nodes and routes should have support through future regulations. These routes are to be defined by 2030 and delivered by 2050. In England it is likely that this role was to have been undertaken by the National Infrastructure Commission, although its role has been downgraded since the referendum. An alternative way of designating these comprehensive networks will be through the transport plans being prepared by Transport for the North and the Midlands Engine, with other major regional scale bodies to follow.

It may be surprising that this work is still being pursued although these routes may only have a local significance subsequently and their designation is one of those potential benefits foregone. However, it is also useful to note that Switzerland, a non-EU member, receives funding from the EU for access and improvements to its transport routes so that surrounding EU member states can move their goods across the European mainland. The UK stands between mainland Europe and Ireland so the UK government may be hoping that if it provides these designated comprehensive routes post Brexit then they may be funded by the EU. Of course the EU also has a strongly supported policy for short sea shipping and this might prove to be more advantageous than travel of goods by road and rail. The EU ports policy is also high on the agenda and again supported by the UK at present.

While transport infrastructure designation and investment has been underway since 1996, a focus on integrated transport plans and programmes has been brought forward through Sustainable Urban Mobility Plans (SUMPs) for FEAs. This initiative was launched in Bristol and is already being developed across a number of UK cities including Brighton and Hove, Bath and North East Somerset, Aberdeen, Belfast, Edinburgh, Glasgow, Leeds, Leicester, London, Milton Keynes, Preston, Wrexham, Norwich, Reading, Southampton and Sunderland.[10] The purposes of these SUMPs will be to improve the accessibility of urban areas and provide high-quality and sustainable mobility and transport to, through and within the urban area. It regards the needs of the 'functioning city' and its hinterland rather than a municipal administrative region.[11]

Another reason why the government may be focusing on these projects for comprehensive networks, ports and SUMPs could be to ensure that the Department for Transport can make a strong claim for replacement funds post Brexit. It could also be that the department is hedging its bets and it may have decided that behaving in a compliant manner in the current period could mean that, should the UK remain in a relevant relationship within the EU, it will still be able to receive funds.

[10] www.eltis.org/mobility-plans
[11] www.eltis.org/mobility-plans/sump-concept

The EU is also progressing the interoperability of railways across the EU through the Railway Package; this looks at ways in which EU railways can have the same financial reporting and funding mechanisms in place.[12]

Spatial plans and territorial policies

One of the major features of the next EU programme cycle will be developing a new strategic and spatial plan for the union's territory. This will be based on the principles of social and economic cohesion, together with that of territorial cohesion, which was added to the founding principles through the Lisbon Treaty.

The EC has attempted to draw up a spatial plan for Europe before, between 1992 and 1999 – the European Spatial Development Perspective (ESDP).[13] This was not formally adopted because the UK disputed the EU's powers for territorial and planning matters. Instead this ESDP was prepared under the auspices of an informal Council of Ministers and adopted by all. At the same time, the EU funded a compendium[14] of planning systems and legislation for each member state in the EU to support the work on the single market and provide access for professionals and investors more easily across member state borders.

This question about the EC's powers for territorial matters was not in dispute with other member states but did drive the EC to clarify and confirm the powers that it had for policy initiation and

[12] European Parliament Think Tank (2016) 'The Railway Package: A Europe without Borders', 28 November, www.europarl.europa.eu/thinktank/en/document.html?reference=IPOL_ATA(2016)576012

[13] European Commission (1999) *European Spatial Development Perspective: Towards Balanced and Sustainable Development of the Territory of the European Union*, http://ec.europa.eu/regional_policy/sources/docoffic/official/reports/pdf/sum_en.pdf

[14] European Commission (2000) 'The EU compendium of spatial planning systems and policies', Regional development studies 28, www.espace-project.org/publications/EUCompendiumUK.pdf

implementation, which were included in the Lisbon Treaty 2007. Since these powers were agreed, their first manifestation was in the bringing together of the EU's cohesion programmes for sub-state areas from 2014 onwards. The EC has also commissioned an update of the compendium for planning systems during the current programme period.[15]

The work on taking forward and integrating these spatial planning programmes as the basis of an investment plan to include the core and comprehensive transport networks, key cities and the strategic programmes of the FEAs across Europe have all started to be brought together within the consideration of future territorial options for the EU.[16] Another component of this work is the EU wide industrial strategy, which has stimulated the UK's own industrial strategy and will feed into its work as long as the UK remains an EU member. The development for this strategy and programme also moves further towards the EC's goals of focusing on places and scales of government for its programmes rather than the existing silos of sectors based on the different directorates general within the EC. Other components that will be added to this are the outcome of Energy Europe and TEN-E and the development and application of the Juncker investment plan for Europe. This approach will also implement the results of the UN Climate Change agreement and the New Urban Agenda agreed in Quito at Habitat III.[17]

On leaving the EU, what will the effects of not being part of this European spatial development and investment plan be? In the short term, this plan will provide an indication of future investment in infrastructure and to some extent an indication of FEAs and major cities. It will be the basis of further developing the circular economy

---

[15] ESPON, 'Comparative Analysis of Territorial Governance and Spatial Planning Systems in Europe', www.espon.eu/main/Menu_Projects/Menu_AppliedResearch/07.GovernanceandSpatialPlanning.html

[16] ESPON, 'Possible European Territorial Futures', www.espon.eu/main/Menu_Projects/Menu_AppliedResearch/06.TerritorialFutures.html

[17] United Nations (2016) 'The New Urban Agenda', https://habitat3.org/the-new-urban-agenda/

and the delivery of UN agendas for climate change. It will also identify projects to be supported and locations that will be potentially suitable and attractive for private investment based on the level of certainty and public sector investment supported by this plan. For the UK, the designation of network routes may not match or link with the key routes and cities in the UK. In the past, the east–west focus of TEN-T has lead to major investment as the UK is an important link for freight movements between Ireland and mainland Europe. The new TEN-T network corridors designated in 2013 are primarily north–south in their orientation. Following Brexit, these will end in France or Spain and will be focused on links with Ireland. The UK ports may also need new facilities for handling customs and checking imports. Those UK ports that have international handling facilities, such as London Gateway, may be more advantaged than others that have a primarily EU focus currently, such as Dover and Harwich.

While any EU plan and programme provides certainty for public and private investment, will it have any direct effects in the UK? The immediate consequences might be experienced in England where, unlike Scotland, Wales and Northern Ireland, there is no national strategic spatial plan and there is continued uncertainty about longer-term infrastructure investment. The strategic planning powers for directly elected city mayors in England may provide some certainty within FEAs. This may be increased through the meso regions identified as the Northern Powerhouse, Midlands Engine and other smaller areas that are likely to follow. These are also being supported by new transport authorities, such as Transport for the North[18] and the Midlands Connect. However, there are also no UK strategic plans that join up national routes and investment priorities and this may serve to suck the energy and life out of potential investment in the UK in comparison with mainland Europe and Ireland.

[18] Transport for the North, www.transportforthenorth.com; HM Government, 'The Midlands Engine for Growth: Prospectus', www.gov.uk/government/uploads/system/uploads/attachment_data/file/482247/midlands-engine-for-growth.pdf

There will be other losses as part of this new strategic plan such as the proposed future approaches for ports.[19] The EU has prioritised short sea shipping as a means of replacing road transport and alongside this the development and improvement of ports. The EC is currently considering a range of port initiatives including the designation of maritime clusters that create specialised services and ancillary industries and can also be of support to their hinterlands. This is expected to require regeneration and investment to achieve these links. The EC has also identified ports as key connecting points for energy production and transmission, including for offshore wind production. Finally, ports can also be main attractors for tourists, and support recreation that can be a considerable addition to the local economy. The EC has identified the need for port master plans to draw together the key actors and to bring forward a strategic approach for the land and sea, and also for the transport connections and other infrastructure connections that are required to make them successful.[20]

Environment and climate change policies

One of the key areas where the EU has provided agreement on policies, programmes and legislation has been the environment. The EU was an energetic participant in 2015 Climate Change agreement in Paris and has prioritised the actions for its implementation at the subsequent meeting in Marrakesh.[21] Following this the EU is seeking to reform its emissions trading scheme post 2020. The proposal introduces a new limit on greenhouse gas emissions to achieve the EU climate targets

---

[19] European Commission, 'Ports', https://ec.europa.eu/transport/modes/maritime/ports/ports_en

[20] European Parliament (2016) 'Briefing: EU port cities and port area regeneration', November, www.europarl.europa.eu/RegData/etudes/BRIE/2016/593500/EPRS_BRI(2016)593500_EN.pdf

[21] European Parliament News (2016) 'COP22 in Marrakesh: "EU will deliver on commitments whatever happens"', 18 November, www.europarl.europa.eu/news/en/news-room/20161114STO51118/cop22-in-marrakesh-eu-will-deliver-on-commitments-whatever-happens

for 2030, new rules for addressing carbon leakage, and provisions for funding innovation and modernisation in the energy sector. It will also encourage member states to compensate for indirect carbon costs.[22]

Although the future direction for environmental policy in the UK will be located in the UN Paris Climate Change agreement, the UK will still need to develop legislation to ensure that these treaty obligations are fulfilled in ways that can be openly demonstrated. The initial concern will be that the UK has the appropriate skill base in government to do this in the future. However, this may not be an issue depending on which form of Brexit agreement the UK negotiates, given that compliance to environmental standards and policies will form part of any UK access to the single market or though the customs union or free trade area. If none of these apply, the trade agreements that the UK has with the WTO will also need to be compliant with UN treaty obligations. The UK Parliament has also prioritised an investigation into the ways that climate change issues will be addressed in the forthcoming UK industrial strategy.[23]

The net effect of all of these contextual pressures may be that the UK adopts the policy and legislation developed in the EU as the most efficient and practical form of implementation. There will, however, be some differences. The level and monitoring of compliance of environmental standards within the UK will no longer be undertaken by the EC where failure to deliver to designated standards can lead to an escalation of the issue to the European Court of Justice and has resulted in the UK paying considerable fines in the past on issues such as bathing water, air quality, waste and EIA (Environmental Impact Assessment). After Brexit, citizens will no longer be able to apply to the

---

[22] European Parliament Think Tank (2016) 'Post-2020 reform of the EU Emissions Trading System', 28 October, www.europarl.europa.eu/thinktank/en/document.html?reference=EPRS_BRI(2016)593498

[23] Business, Energy and Industrial Strategy Committee (2016) 'Leaving the EU: negotiation priorities for energy and climate change policy inquiry', www.parliament.uk/business/committees/committees-a-z/commons-select/business-energy-industrial-strategy/inquiries/parliament-2015/brexit-energy-climate-change-inquiry-16-17/

EU to enforce environmental standards. On air quality, the government was recently found to be acting illegally and has been forced to bring forward its air quality strategy much more rapidly than it wished.[24] In future, UK citizens will have to rely on UK legislation for these matters while the EU is now updating its air quality standards.[25]

The UK Parliament is also concerned about these issues and is already asking the government about its intended vision for the environment post Brexit and whether it foresees any changes in policy direction on leaving the EU.[26] The role of EU policy, programmes and legislation in providing frameworks for each nation in the UK as part of the devolved settlement will also need to be considered. The UK Parliament is also interested in what the UK's future relationship with the EU will look like with regards to environment and climate change policy and whether there would be business benefits of aligning UK with EU environmental policy. On the other hand, the Committee has asked if there are benefits in adopting different environmental standards to the EU and whether this would reduce any related administrative burdens. The UK Parliament is also aware that there are environmental standards included in the trade deals that the EU has with third party countries to which the UK may continue to have access.

---

[24] Carrington, D. (2016) 'High court rules UK government plans to tackle air pollution are illegal', *Guardian*, 2 November, www.theguardian.com/environment/2016/nov/02/high-court-rules-uk-government-plans-to-tackle-air-pollution-are-illegal

[25] European Parliament Think Tank (2016) 'National emission ceilings for air pollutants', 15 November, www.europarl.europa.eu/thinktank/en/document.html?reference=EPRS_ATA(2016)593526

[26] Lords Select Committee (2016) 'What is the Government's vision for environment and climate change policy post-Brexit?', 9 November, www.parliament.uk/business/committees/committees-a-z/lords-select/eu-energy-environment-subcommittee/news-parliament-2015/ministers-env-cc-brexit/

Economic policy

The membership of the EU including of its single market still has the potential to grow with negotiations currently being conducted with Montenegro, Serbia and Turkey. Albania and the Former Yugoslav Republic of Macedonia are also candidate countries, while Bosnia and Herzegovina and Kosovo are potential candidate countries. Each candidate country has to satisfy specific requirements before it can be accepted as a full member of the EU and these include practice of government, regulation, trade and rights but also depends on the EU's institutional capacity for enlargement. This includes the balance of voting rights within the European Council and the membership of the European Parliament as well as staff members of the EC.

The increase in cross border transfer of goods and services in the single market is also a policy area where further work is being undertaken to improve internal trade within the EU. The EU is prompting further work on civil law that has to ensure a high degree of legal certainty for citizens in cross border relations, to guarantee citizens easy and effective access to civil justice in order to settle cross border disputes and to simplify cross border cooperation instruments between national civil courts.

One of the key areas that will not be open to the UK if it is outside the single market will be the opportunity to bid for and receive tenders for public sector work. The process of public procurement in the EU was reformed in 2014, in an attempt to make tenders more accessible for small firms.

In addition to the benefits of the widening market, the EU is also cracking down on tax havens. At present the UK is fighting against the inclusion of Jersey, Guernsey, the Isle of Man, Bermuda and the Cayman Islands on its blacklist. The EC consider that a zero or near-zero rate of corporation tax in a non-EU country should be a red flag for 'unfair taxation' but member states including the UK are resisting this definition.

The EU has an industrial strategy that is focused on helping existing industry to transition to be more productive and efficient and in 2014 the EC launched 'For a European Industrial Renaissance' (COM (2014) 0014), which focuses on reversing industrial decline and reaching the target of 20% of GDP for manufacturing activities by 2020. Beyond this the EC states that in order to attract new investments and create a better business environment, the EU needs more coherent politics in the field of the internal market, including European infrastructure such as energy, transport and information networks, as well as for goods and services. Part of this strategy is focused on innovation through the Innovation Union that was established as part of the Europe 2020 programme and has already started work on standards and supporting innovation partnerships. This approach includes the development of the single digital market that is promoting not only innovation but also increases in growth through productivity and efficiency gains.[27] There are also proposals to reform the Common Agricultural Policy after 2020 to improve food security, support rural areas, implement better environmental standards and increase future resilience through land management.[28] For financial services, the UK will lose its passporting rights if it is not part of the single market although it can ask for third country equivalence[29] which operates on a piecemeal basis, although this is not expected to be sufficiently comprehensive. The UK is already requesting a hybrid relationship with the EU on this but it will always lag behind future financial service developments and have to negotiate access to them on a case by case basis. Another area where the EU is supporting changing practices is in the increase on efficiency in the

---

[27] European Parliament (2016) 'Establishing a Skills Guarantee, At a glance', Plenary – 18 November, www.europarl.europa.eu/RegData/etudes/ATAG/2016/593528/EPRS_ATA(2016)593528_EN.pdf

[28] European Parliament, 'Committee of Agriculture and Rural Development', www.europarl.europa.eu/committees/en/agri/home.html; European Parliament Think Tank (2016) 'The CAP and job creation in rural areas', 19 October, www.europarl.europa.eu/thinktank/en/document.html?reference=EPRS_ATA(2016)589840

[29] European Parliament (2016) 'Briefing: Third-country equivalence in EU banking legislation', PE 587.369, 9 December, www.europarl.europa.eu/RegData/etudes/BRIE/2016/587369/IPOL_BRI(2016)587369_EN.pdf

public sector and the future EU budget rounds will seek to integrate these reforms further into programmes and processes.[30]

One of the main objectives of the EU is promoting economic activity and employment. Since the economic crisis, there have been higher levels of unemployment across all member states with the lowest levels being in Germany and the UK. Higher levels of unemployment have prevailed in Italy, Greece and Spain. The EU is also concerned with the distribution of unemployment within member states in specific regions. The EU has adopted a skills guarantee that will set in place national pathways for skills development and training, which will be monitored.[31]

The programmes established by the EU will be lost to the UK on Brexit, together with developmental approaches to creating more job opportunities for those who are unemployed. Unlike many programmes developed for lagging regions by the UK before it joined the EU, the EU's approach is more comprehensive and covers the whole of the territory of member states. The EU wants to see how these initiatives can combine together to achieve change. In the period beyond 2020, the EU is already starting to focus on what will be required as part of the UN's Habitat III New Urban Agenda, which brings together economic and social ambitions for lagging and underperforming areas.

Social and cultural policy

EU social and cultural policy crosses all types of areas and peoples. The future of EU policy for rural areas after 2020 is under consideration. The development of rural strategy and support has been growing within the EU since the McSharry reforms in 1992 and each subsequent programme period has developed more cohesive

---

[30] European Parliament Think Tank (2016) 'Public Sector Reform: How the EU Budget Is Used to Encourage it', 31 August, www.europarl.europa.eu/thinktank/en/document.html?reference=IPOL_STU(2016)572696

[31] European Parliament (2016) 'Establishing a Skills Guarantee'.

approaches to considering the best ways to provide support. These current considerations about the future of rural areas are addressing a number of issues including the relationships between urban and rural areas, and the need of the EU to further engage in rural development, recognising that rural areas are different. Future thinking is also considering ways in which support can be more effective to promote rural innovation and 'vitality'. There is also an understanding of the need to address rural poverty. These rural development initiatives sit alongside the direct payments made to farmers for environment and land management. These payments are likely to move more in the direction of supporting biodiversity, biomass and climate change in the future with an emphasis on ecological resilience. It is also recognised that in the longer term the current direct payments model will not be able to continue and instead there should be focused payments to achieve specific outcomes for food production or wider environmental issues. Moreover, all EU payments should be conditional on at least some identified environmental benefits.

Since the Treaty of Lisbon 2007, the EC has been able to take a more direct interest in public health and is particularly focusing on prevention and promoting healthy lifestyles by addressing the issues of nutrition, physical activity, alcohol, tobacco and drug consumption, environmental risks and injuries. There is also a concern for ageing and helping member states' healthcare systems respond to these challenges. Finally, the EU is concerned with protecting citizens from health threats including epidemics and bioterrorism and with increasing capacity to respond to new health challenges such as climate change. In future there is an expectation that this public health work will be more integrated with other EU programmes, including those for the environment, transport, agriculture and economic development. Further policies and active support can be expected after the UK is likely to leave the EU.

Energy policy

The issues affecting energy and the security of supply have increased in recent years. The dependence of EU member states on supplies from Russia has meant that many countries could be held to ransom if their energy supplies were removed or stopped as Russia has done in Ukraine. It also means that member states are dependent on supply at prices that can be varied and over which they have no control. Other energy supplies come from oil that is supplied at agreements through OPEC and at spot prices that are agreed each day. These may go up and down and in order to stabilise energy prices, including that of oil, companies dependent on energy frequently insure their supply at a specific price for a fixed period using hedging.

The EU has been undertaking a range of measures to improve the certainty of supply and has a major initiative, Energy Europe. Through this a number of programmes have been developed. The first is the crafting of a cross EU energy grid that includes the UK not least as it is on the pathway between Ireland and the EU. Through this grid the EU is also attempting secure supplies from third party countries such as Norway to counterbalance the potential risk in Russian supply. The EU is developing an approach to local energy production through a range of mechanisms using water, heat pumps and photovoltaic cells that can be fed back into the grid as well as supplying energy to communities.

The EU has a smart metering project across the EU that has a priority to encourage households to manage their use of energy at point of delivery and to switch between sources if this is more efficient. This is being rolled out in the UK although in ways that do not fulfil the spirit of the scheme. Each energy supplier is providing a smart meter rather than one for all energy supplied and they are being connected via mobile phone systems. This means that as many meters are located in basements of properties, there is no mobile phone signal, the meters cannot therefore function and they are not easily accessible for daily monitoring by the householder as was intended. The roll out in the UK is also behind schedule deadlines. This approach to delivery of EU agreed policies in the UK is typical of an approach in UK government that has not embraced the purpose intended and has misread or mistransposed legislation in order not to challenge existing institutional responsibilities and working practices. It also reflects the reduced importance and understanding of the role of public services in England with a greater focus on market providers' concerns than the wider issues to be dealt with, such as energy consumption. This is particularly an issue in the UK where energy is under stress following a failure of UK officials to understand the application of EU legislation on air quality and the use of carbon fuels from the early 1990s onwards.

The provision of energy is also related to other environmental objectives including clean air and the role of pollutants. In 1990, the EU indicated that new higher standards would apply to energy plans that were reliant on coal and gas. Unfortunately, the UK did not take appropriate heed of these forthcoming changes and over 2012–20 power stations will be taken out of supply within the UK.

The EU has played a leading role in promoting renewable energy and adopted its latest action in 2009.[32] It is currently reviewing the programme after 2020 which will deal with the role of renewable energy within the main EU energy markets. The EU has started preparing for the period beyond 2020, in order to provide early policy clarity for investors. Renewable energy plays a key part in the Commission's long-term strategy as outlined in its 'Energy Roadmap 2050' (COM (2011) 0885). The decarbonisation scenarios for the energy sector proposed in the roadmap point to a renewable energy share of at least 30% by 2030. However, the roadmap also suggests that the growth of renewable energy will slacken after 2020 unless there is further intervention. Following the publication in March 2013 of a green paper entitled 'A 2030 framework for climate and energy policies' (COM (2013) 0169), the Commission, in its communication of 22 January 2014 entitled 'A policy framework for climate and energy in the period from 2020 to 2030' (COM (2014) 0015), proposed not

[32] 2009 Directive on Renewable Energy, http://eur-lex.europa.eu/legal-content/EN/ALL/?uri=CELEX%3A32009L0028

to renew binding national targets for renewable energy after 2020. A mandatory target – 27% of energy consumption to come from renewable sources – is provided for only at EU level. The Commission expects nationally binding greenhouse gas emission targets to spur growth in the energy sector.[33]

Finally, the UK Government has also signalled that it wishes to withdraw from EURATOM as well as EU membership. This was a treaty made in 1957 to support the creation of a market for nuclear power and promoting safety and research. The treaty establishing EURATOM is distinct from that for the EU although its membership is the same with the addition of Switzerland in 2014.

[33] European Parliament Think Tank (2016) 'Renewable energy', 1 September, www.europarl.europa.eu/thinktank/en/document.html?reference=04A_FT(2013)050704

EIGHT

How can we assess the future beyond Brexit?

The changing context for Brexit

2016 has been a year of surprises that were seemingly unpredictable before they occurred and easier to understand with the benefit of hindsight. People have expressed their desire for change in the UK and the US through their votes, preferring to take a chance on the unknown rather than voting for the safety of continuity and experience. A new set of rules for political behaviour has emerged that appeals to emotions rather than expert advice and where politicians can change minds in a new era of 'post-truth' politics. In these elections, many people who had not voted for many years decided to participate in a bid for disruptive change and were willing to take a gamble that this would bring more focus on their position as those frequently left behind or marginalised. It also offered an opportunity for older people to vote for a past sense of stability and order that they felt was gone and for some elites to promote the free market without regulation under the guise of restoring sovereignty. President Trump's tweet to the UK government to suggest that the then interim UKIP leader Nigel Farage should be the new UK Ambassador in the US is one example of how protocols and working practices have been dumped.

Advisors are seen as part of the establishment opposition preventing change with their longstanding and weighed advice.

The negotiations for the UK's future in the EU enter this changing frame of reference. Any outcome seems possible in this future. This book has identified the many options and potential outcomes of this process, which remains complex and politically charged. The UK's departure from the EU will leave it much weakened in a post-Trump world, despite his German and Scottish ancestry. Trump's election gives no particular succour to the UK which, despite the Prime Minister's early meeting with the US President, had relied on continuing support from the US. Trump's new political deal making will be based on the kind of brinkmanship that is the anathema of the career diplomat and civil servant and some of its consequences – intended or otherwise – may be unlikely and unpredictable.

It has always been in the US' interest for the UK to remain within the EU. If the new President comes to this view will he make the UK a deal – we change our position on the EU in return for continuing defence and security cover for example? In a new 'America First' approach to trade, the UK can no longer necessarily rely on the volume of its exports going to a single country. The US might suggest some kind of arrangement that gives the UK access to its markets post-Brexit but the price may be too high in what is expected, such as reducing environmental and food standards, opening the NHS to US business or more widely giving up the UK's position on the UN Security Council in favour of a pro Trump member. What is clear from this new US deal making is that it will stretch across all policy areas and not be confined within specific spheres or sectors. This will require new diplomatic skills and there may be little past experience to rely on except learning from the ways that the US President has brokered some of his previous business deals.

This issue of the changing world and increase in popularism cannot be ignored and forms a contextual envelope for all that will follow in the UK's negotiations with the EU. It has already been suggested that the UK's unwritten constitution is not strong enough to cope with the future.[1] This changing world and rising popularism will inform and shape Brexit in ways that cannot be anticipated. This chapter discusses some of the overarching questions that need to be considered in the coming months and years as the UK and the EU make their way through a political minefield that could result in the breakup of the EU and UK.

Will the Brexit process influence the outcome?

The UK referendum on EU membership was a simple in/out question but subsequently there is a greater understanding of the range of agreements that it has through the EU and the complexities of the exit process, including the issues and options to be considered. The first issue is that the majority was clear but small and, although there was a large electoral turnout, in effect only 33% of the UK population voted to leave the EU. Second, although there was a political commitment from the Prime Minister for the referendum to be put into effect whatever the result, the referendum was not legally binding. Third, there have been concerns about the legitimacy of the claims made in the campaign of the leave group and these have been referred to the Crown Prosecution Service – for example that leaving the EU would not effect EU funding to localities.[2] There are also concerns about how the process is triggered. The Supreme Court found that Parliament must pass legislation to give power to the Government to invoke Article 50 of the 2007 Lisbon Treaty. The focus is now on the role of Parliament at all stages of any process. A further issue has been raised on whether triggering Article 50 also means that the UK will leave the EEA, which includes the UK in the single market, which is covered by separate agreements. A judicial review was unsuccessfully launched

[1] Barnett, A. (2016) 'Why Britain needs a written constitution', *Guardian*, 30 November, www.theguardian.com/commentisfree/2016/nov/30/why-britain-needs-written-constitution

[2] BBC News (2016) 'Welsh EU cash 'maintained' after Brexit, say vote Leave', 14 June, www.bbc.co.uk/news/uk-wales-politics-36523232

to determine whether the UK is empowered to trigger Article 127 of the EEA agreement without specific parliamentary authority. It has also been suggested by former Deputy Prime Minister Nick Clegg that the German government had been proposing to provide a deal on free movement issues for the UK on the basis of continued association through the EEA.[3] The Prime Minister has ruled out any form of membership of the EU in her own principles for future UK/EU relationships[4] although this may be modified through the process of negotiation and Parliamentary agreements.

The role of Parliament in the negotiation process is central and, as the House of Lords pointed out, under the initial arrangements the opportunities to engage in the process were less than those opportunities offered to the European Parliament. It has requested parity with the European Parliament within the process, including both the supply of documents and witnesses together with government responses on all the recommendations made by Parliament.[5] This access appears likely to be made in a secure room. Another criticism is that until the Prime Minister's speech on 17 January 2017, the heads of EU member states appeared to have much greater knowledge of the EU's negotiating position than the UK population and Parliament. The Prime Minister held a series of bilateral meetings with other EU member states following which the heads of state have reported back to their colleagues about the UK's position and matters discussed.[6] However, this was in the absence of any briefing in the UK from government. A group of Conservative MPs has written to Donald

---

[3] www.qmul.ac.uk/media/news/items/hss/191708.html

[4] www.gov.uk/government/speeches/the-governments-negotiating-objectives-for-exiting-the-eu-pm-speech

[5] House of Lords European Union Committee (2016) 'Brexit: parliamentary scrutiny', 4th Report of Session 2016–17, www.publications.parliament.uk/pa/ld201617/ldselect/ldeucom/50/50.pdf

[6] Henley, J. and Walker, P. (2016) 'Britain may not be ready to trigger article 50 by April, says Malta's PM', *Guardian*, 25 November, www.theguardian.com/politics/2016/nov/25/britain-not-ready-trigger-article-50-april-brexit-malta-pm

Tusk, President of the EU Council, requesting certainty for the position of UK nationals living in the EU and was met by a reply that the uncertainty is of the UK's making and this, like other matters, would have to wait until Article 50 has been triggered.[7]

Following the Supreme Court judgement on 24 January[8] the government introduced a Bill in Parliament to invoke Article 50 on 26 January.[9] Then there are considerations of the UK's preferred outcome, which may be a key issue in the parliamentary Bill process. As this book has demonstrated, there are many different options to consider and these become more complex as different parts of the UK's 45-year relationship with the EU are examined. What process is required? What new relationships are being sought? How can the UK replace not only the European Communities Act 1972 but also the legislation that it will lose if there is a hard Brexit? The Prime Minister has promised a Great Repeal Bill that will include the re-negotiated arrangements once these have been concluded.[10]

A number of Conservative politicians argued that the Prime Minister should drop the appeal to the Supreme Court, publish a Bill to trigger Article 50 and then get on with the process rather than delaying it.[11] Although not so openly argued, another reason behind this approach was risk management. When a case goes to court on a matter of legal determination, it is better to have some expectation of the outcome. The case going to the Supreme Court has no precedent and therefore the outcome may give Parliament more power than a simple Bill

[7]   Asthana, A. and Mason, R. (2016) 'Donald Tusk blames British voters for expats' EU uncertainty', *Guardian*, 29 November, www.theguardian.com/politics/2016/nov/29/donald-tusk-turns-on-tories-in-row-over-rights-of-eu-citizens-in-uk

[8]   www.supremecourt.uk/news/article-50-brexit-appeal.html

[9]   www.gov.uk/government/news/article-50-bill-process-begins

[10] House of Commons Library (2016) 'Legislating for Brexit: the Great Repeal Bill', 21 November, http://researchbriefings.parliament.uk/ResearchBriefing/Summary/CBP-7793

[11] Hawkins, R. (2016) 'Drop Brexit case appeal, senior Tories urge May', BBC News, 19 November, www.bbc.co.uk/news/uk-politics-38034411

would provide. The absence of any assessment from the government on the likely implications for the Prime Minister's planned outcome or indeed the tradeoffs that will need to be struck is now seen as the product of a political impasse within the Conservative Party[12] and following pressures May agreed to publish a White Paper. While the Prime Minister makes statements about the need to restore social justice and help people who are struggling, she is not reminding people that this is the core principle of the EU and, without membership, the UK will have no legal treaty anchor for the way it seeks to undertake any social, economic and territorial redistribution.

It is also important to consider the role of the main political parties in Parliament. The Conservative Party is split over the Brexit issue but the other parties, apart from the Ulster Unionists, are primarily in favour of remaining in the EU. In the House of Lords, the overwhelming majority of members are in favour of remaining. However, in the country, only the Liberal Democrats are speaking to the electorate about these issues and the Labour Party has been criticised for not offering any effective opposition on the issue or indeed speaking to those anxious about the future.[13] A group of 90 Labour MPs wrote to the *Guardian* on 21 November 2016 saying that hard Brexit would be a disaster for working people, in response to a letter from 60 MPs to the Prime Minister saying that she should leave quickly, which is also the position of UKIP. The Liberal Democrats are promoting the argument for a second referendum and used the by-election in the Richmond constituency to raise this issue. The by-election was

[12] Kettle, M. (2016) 'MPs can see off hard Brexit. The ball is in their court', *Guardian*, 17 November, www.theguardian.com/commentisfree/2016/nov/17/mps-hard-brexit-progressives-parliament

[13] Harris, J. (2016) 'On Brexit, the Labour leadership offers anxious voters ... nothing', *Guardian*, 23 November, www.theguardian.com/commentisfree/2016/nov/23/eu-brexit-labour-leadership-article-50; Mason, P. (2016) 'How do we fight the loudmouth politics of authoritarian populism?', *Guardian*, 21 November, www.theguardian.com/commentisfree/2016/nov/21/how-do-we-fight-loudmouth-politics-authoritarianism-populism-paul-mason

caused by the resignation of the sitting Conservative MP over the government's decision to expand Heathrow.

Outside Parliament, politicians and former Prime Ministers are also starting to campaign in a more organised way for remaining in the EU. The British Influence group comprised of politicians across all parties has started to increase its visibility and campaign through its support for the EEA Article 127 case. The former Prime Minister Tony Blair has been holding talks with others including another former Prime Minister John Major and former Deputy Prime Minister Nick Clegg. Blair is proposing to open a new think tank and organisation to promote remain. The European Movement pressure group has elected a new chair, Stephen Dorrell, and is campaigning on various key issues.[14] The former Prime Minister Gordon Brown has proposed a federal solution for the future of the UK and Richard Branson is proposing to fund a campaign to support remain initiatives. The start of 2017 may find a considerable increase of campaigning for the UK to remain in the EU.

On the Brexit side, the statements for those in favour of a hard Brexit position have started to increase the stridency of their statements. Nigel Farage suggested that there would be a mass demonstration if the Supreme Court judges did not find in favour of the government although this did not occur. The appeal of the hard Brexit group is to the will of the people but this phrase is becoming overused as the UK appreciates that this is a more difficult and a potentially destabilising set of actions. The 'will of the people' is also a slogan of popularism[15] and suggests that the democratically ruling elites are against them. This othering has been identified as the technique used in the Trump electoral campaign.[16]

[14] https://euromove.org.uk/

[15] Cohen, N. (2016) 'What has become of conservatism?', *Guardian*, 27 November, www.theguardian.com/commentisfree/2016/nov/27/what-has-become-of-conservatism-trump-farage-le-pen-brexit

[16] Weigel, M. (2016) 'Political correctness: how the right invented a phantom enemy', The long read, *Guardian*, 30 November, www.theguardian.com/us-news/2016/nov/30/political-correctness-how-the-right-invented-phantom-enemy-donald-trump

Any agreement for a continuing relationship between the UK and the EU is likely to involve payments from the UK. This is a model that is used between the EU and other states and the UK will have financial commitments to the EU that will extend beyond membership.[17] It will mean that the UK will lose its rebate and will have no significant input into decision and law making. Parts of the UK are also examining whether they can maintain relationships through Ireland[18] and, although this might be possible for specific projects and initiatives, it will not cover the majority of issues that are currently jointly decided within the EU.

What will be the effects of Brexit on the UK economy?

In examining what the effects of Brexit will be on the UK economy, it is important to have some idea about which model might be favoured. These are set out in Chapter Three and daily there are different reports of conversations from cabinet ministers about the government's favoured options. The Foreign Secretary Boris Johnson told the Czech Prime Minister that the UK would like to leave the customs union and the Brexit Minister told members of the European Parliament that the UK still favoured membership of the single market if this could be achieved. While the Prime Minister has published her twelve objectives for the negotiations, that include certainty, protecting workers' rights and free trade with the EU together with a continuing relationship on security,[19] this will cause increasing challenges for the UK economy. The Prime Minister has given the Confederation

---

[17] Johnston, C. (2016) 'UK will have EU bills after Brexit, German finance minister says', *Guardian*, 18 November, www.theguardian.com/politics/2016/nov/17/german-minister-takes-hard-line-over-britains-eu-commitments-post-brexit

[18] O'Carroll, L. (2016) 'Wales urged to do deal with Ireland to secure EU funds post-Brexit', *Guardian*, 28 November, www.theguardian.com/uk-news/2016/nov/28/wales-urged-to-do-deal-with-ireland-to-secure-eu-funds-post-brexit

[19] www.gov.uk/government/speeches/the-governments-negotiating-objectives-for-exiting-the-eu-pm-speech

of British Industry the assurance that the transition period from the EU to another trading state will take some time – perhaps ten years. However, it may do little to reassure the business community if the period of uncertainty about the UK's trading agreements extends longer than was initially assumed.

The early response of the UK economy following the Brexit referendum result has been mixed. The value of the pound has dropped 15% and the resulting expectation of more tourists has not occurred. The Bank of England secured economic confidence through quantitative easing and the consumer economy seemed to be responding well, possibly on the assumption that 2017 and beyond will see higher prices and more repetitions on credit.

In the medium to long term, the economic situation is less certain. What are the key issues to consider? The first is how many companies will move at least part if not all their operations outside the UK. In the financial services sector, this kind of move is being encouraged by the financial regulator who wishes to see companies protecting the assets that they manage and hold. Although US insurance companies like AIG expect to retain offices and a large staff in the UK, they are preparing to move their headquarters inside the EU area.[20]

The second issue to consider will be wage and price inflation. Price inflation will occur first as the falling pound will start to affect the value of important goods and these goods will be sold at higher prices even if retailers manage to contain some of the increases. The increase in wage inflation may occur later when it is clear that free movement will end, if this is the outcome negotiated. Since the referendum in June 2016, the volume of migration into the UK from the EU has increased and this has been absorbed into the labour market, with the UK having lower levels of unemployment than for some time. However, if the economies of the Eurozone countries improve, then those coming from other member states may return home to work. Those undertaking

[20] Jones, H. and Cohn, C. (2016) 'AIG joins list of finance firms looking at moving some UK operations', Reuters, 22 November, www.reuters.com/article/us-britain-eu-insurance-idUSKBN13H0U9

more professional roles may take longer to move as they seek specific jobs in other member states. These include academics and medical professionals who may no longer wish to be at risk by remaining within the UK. Some UK citizens currently working in other EU member states may decide to change their citizenship and drop out of the UK population count. Overall, the country is becoming more diverse[21] and less segregated but this leaves those areas isolated by limited transport access feeling less likely to want change.[22]

While the UK Prime Minister has pledged to have the lowest corporation tax to make the UK attractive to companies, this is an area not currently within EU agreements and Hungary[23] has already indicated that it will drop its corporation tax level to below those of Ireland and Cyprus, which are currently the lowest in the EU at 12.5%. If Hungary goes to the level of 10% then other countries may also seek to use these tax rates and the UK's rate may be lowered further in response. The UK may receive more international company locations as a result. There is also a growing expectation that the ability of multinational corporations to operate their companies in countries that have favourable tax rates will be coming to an end and they will have to pay tax on earnings within the state that they were generated. The EU has found that Ireland has used its tax rates to offer state aid to Apple[24] and this may be part of the America First approach in the US.

The UK had also assumed a positive and supportive approach from other countries once it left the EU. Although President Obama stated that the UK would be in the back of the queue in terms of trade deals, relationships between the UK and US following Trump's election may be more focused on defence and security issues. However, it

[21] Catney, G. (2016) 'Britain is becoming more diverse, not more segregated', The Conversation, 17 November,https://theconversation.com/britain-is-becoming-more-diverse-not-more-segregated-68610

[22] Mason (2016).

[23] Rumney, E. (2016) 'Hungary to set lowest EU corporate tax rate from January', Public Finance International, 18 November, www.publicfinanceinternational.org/news/2016/11/hungary-set-lowest-eu-corporate-tax-rate-january

[24] http://europa.eu/rapid/press-release_IP-16-2923_en.htm

is uncertain what kind of trade deals would be offered from other countries. Having concluded the new CETA between Canada and the EU, the Canadian Prime Minister Trudeau has said that Canada has no priority to arrange a trade deal with the UK.

What pressures will be placed on the EU by international bodies to close the gap with the UK?

In the immediate aftermath of the result of the UK referendum, international financial bodies including the IMF and the World Bank urged the UK and the EU to consider the extent of the profound shock on the world's economic position if the UK leaves the EU. Beyond this, there appears to have been behind the scenes discussions and pressure placed on the EU to make its negotiating stance more flexible to allow the UK some improved terms. If this flexibility does occur, it will be after the round of elections in EU member states that will be held during 2017.

How will Brexit affect the whole of the UK?

The outcome of the negotiations between the EU and the UK could have considerable repercussions for the future of the UK. The Scottish First Minister has stated the need to reaffirm Scotland's future in Europe and is considering all means to retain access to the single market and the free movement of people. The Scottish government has published *Scotland: A European Nation*.[25] In this, the potential losses to working rights, and the reduction in environmental standards and renewable energy are identified as key threats to Scotland if the UK leaves the EU. Scotland is also identified culturally as being part of Europe through the Enlightenment and its history before it joined England, Wales

---

[25] Scottish Government (2016) 'Scotland; A European Nation', 21 November, http://news.gov.scot/news/scotland-a-european-nation; Scottish Government (2016) *Scotland: A European Nation*, http://www.gov.scot/Resource/0051/00510265.pdf

and Ireland to form the UK, including its Claim of Right 1689, a foundational law in Scotland's constitution. The publication also sets out which of the Scottish government's powers are located in EU law and those that are retained by the UK government. Of those powers that are devolved, the majority are those agreed by the UK within the EU and the foundational legislation for Scot's devolution sets out the right of the Scottish Parliament to implement these. It sets out the implications for Scotland of Brexit on these devolved powers, undermining its devolved structures and decision making. Finally, there is legislation covering the legislative consent process between the UK and Scottish Parliaments where the UK Parliament cannot legislate to do anything that is devolved to Scotland's Parliament and against its will.

There are therefore doubts about whether the UK as a state can survive Brexit. Former Prime Minister Gordon Brown and Deputy Prime Minister Michael Heseltine have argued for a future federal settlement for the UK in a bid to save the union. This formalisation of powers and decision making between the four nations would go further than the current devolution powers and would give a formal devolved government for England. This might be based in some way on the model of directly elected mayors now being created for combined authorities of both urban and rural areas. From the perspective of Whitehall, Scotland, Wales and Northern Ireland have been regarded as other and not in the 'beltway' of Westminster; but the referendum has demonstrated that England, other than London, Oxford and Cambridge, is different from the rest of the UK and is now the other in this union.[26]

[26] Hassan, G. (2016) 'The UK as we know it can't survive Brexit and Trump', *Guardian*, 17 November, www.theguardian.com/commentisfree/2016/nov/17/britain-brexit-trump-scotland-northern-ireland-wales

How will the EU change without the UK?

Even before the EU referendum, the EU has been under pressure to change. It is primarily a rule bound organisation that is generally effective when dealing with 28 member states. However, it does not work as well when there are crises and a need to agree a more immediate response. The EU has been criticised for being remote and undemocratic although the European Parliament, which is directly elected, has considerably more power in co-decision making than it had initially.

A major pressure on the EU to consider its future comes from the changing political consensus in the US and the rise of popularism in Europe. In the US, the EU has always had an ally in defence and security, although alongside a frequent difference of opinion in terms of trade and liberalism of markets. The development of the Transatlantic Trade and Investment Partnership (TTIP) was one means of developing a joint approach between the largest economies in the world. The pressure to achieve such an agreement was derived from the rise of China and the other BRICS nations and a firmer agreement between western countries was seen to be a means of countering this. A similar relationship in the Trans Pacific Trading Agreement that excluded China was also seen to be a means of strengthening trading alliances between the members of the OECD.

The rise in popularism or nationalism in many EU member states and the US has been a response to the growing trade liberalisation since the WTO Agreement in 1979 on Government Procurement on opening public services to competition.[27] This has manifested itself in many ways from the left-behind towns in the post industrial rust belt of the US, the welfare dependent communities in northern England and the failure to 'punish' the bankers after their profligacy and resulting economic collapse in 2007. Although there might be benefits of cheaper goods made in China and India, these left behind

---

[27] www.wto.org/english/tratop_e/gproc_e/gp_gpa_e.htm

communities would rather have jobs. They also would like to see companies paying taxes to the countries where they make their profits.

Once the UK leaves the EU, then the EU will no longer be the largest global market, ceding that position to the US although there may be a challenge from China for that position in the coming decade. If the EU wishes to retain its trust and confidence with its people, it will have to take a new approach.[28] One that has been suggested by Benjamin Barber is the replacement of states in the EU by functional economic areas run by mayors. He argues that in these new spaces the directly elected mayor can be more in touch with their people and there can be better trade dynamics within and between them.[29] What effects would this have on the UK?

A second area where EU policy is likely to change will be in that of security and defence.[30] Concerns about the growing repositioning of Russia and a potential alliance between the US and Turkey and Russia on its borders may evoke a specific response. In the past the US has been a strong NATO power and this has been supported by the military expenditure and support of the UK. However, President Trump has questioned the US's commitment to NATO and stated that all members of NATO should pay their own way. The UK Prime Minister has also agreed that NATO member states should contribute more. The EU does not have a standing army or a defence policy, not least because the UK has been against it while in membership. Once the UK leaves the EU it would be possible for these initiatives to progress. It is also important to note that if Scotland remains in the EU in some way, it will not contribute soldiers as it does to the current UK army and this may be an important future issue for the UK. The

---

[28] Kettle (2016).

[29] www.ted.com/talks/benjamin_barber_why_mayors_should_rule_the_world; Barber B. (2013) *If Mayors Ruled the World: Dysfunctional Nations, Rising Cities*, New Haven, CT: Yale University Press.

[30] European Parliament News (2016) 'Defence: MEPs push for more EU cooperation to better protect Europe', 23 November, www.europarl.europa. eu/news/en/news-room/20161117IPR51547/defence-meps-push-for-more-eu-cooperation-to-better-protect-europe

EU is also concerned about the rise of terrorism and how to protect itself against the kinds of attacks that have been made in France and Belgium. This suggests greater cooperation on security policy.

The third area of potential change within the EU is the relative power balance between member states. Germany and France as founder members and the largest countries have always had a predominant position. If the UK leaves the EU, then countries such as Poland would expect to have a greater say in the discussions, based on their population size. It might also alter the positions on specific issues such as trade and external focus. The informal operating blocs within the EU might become more formalised and exert more pressure on decision making. There would also be less funding available to provide support for new members and this may cause internal problems. It would also reduce the ability of the EC to negotiate potential deals if there are fewer resources available to achieve this.

Overall, there is a recognition by its leaders that the EU needs to change, but is concerned about enforced changes that might be a consequence of Brexit. This means that the climate for the negotiations is tough and intransigent.[31] This is to discourage others, including the voters in Italy, Austria, France, the Netherlands and Germany where there are important elections in the period to the end of 2017. Once these are concluded, the EU will take stock and if it has managed to come through this period without major changes in the other political leadership of member states then it may be more generous towards the UK. If there have been moves to the populalist right in some of these elections, then the EU may need to respond more rapidly than would normally be its preferred approach. This might suggest a major shift in the four freedoms and an outward and visible confirmation of the shift away from economic liberalisation.[32]

[31] Henley, H., Elgot, J. and Rankin, J. (2016) 'Luxembourg PM tells Britain: either you're in the EU or you're not', *Guardian*, 29 November, www.theguardian.com/politics/2016/nov/29/luxembourg-pm-tells-britain-either-in-the-eu-or-not-xavier-bettel

[32] *Financial Times* (2016) 'Wolfgang Schäuble sets out tough line on Brexit', www.ft.com/content/765a1f2a-acba-11e6-9cb3-bb8207902122

Is it possible to identify any likely unintended consequences?

It is hard to consider the nature of unintended consequences beyond the understanding that there will be some. Before the EU referendum campaign, the UK knew very little about what agreements had been made with the EU, the processes adopted for making them and their transposition into UK law. The common view was that the only relationship between the EU and UK was the single market but subsequently issues such as transport, the environment, health, wider trade, the relationship between universities and EU funded research and the position of UK citizens living in other EU member states have risen to the fore. The popular press has frequently carried stories about EU or Brussels rules being imposed on the UK without any UK knowledge or participation in decision making – this has never been true and in the review of the UK's participation in EU decision making, the UK has rarely used its veto or voted against a decision. A similar lack of knowledge has been displayed in the broadcast media.

The debates about which path to take in negotiations have meant not only that the public has a better understanding of the relationships between the EU and the UK but also the media and civil society. One of the unintended consequences of this period is that all involved will have a much greater understanding of the way in which the EU works than has been available over the last 45 years. There may also be some realisation that the failure to engage with EU processes and discussions in a more open way in the UK has brought about the current division in the country.

The pressure placed on the civil service in the face of the complexity of the discussions and preparations for negotiations following the triggering of Article 50 will be particularly challenging. This is because the Whitehall civil service has primarily been antagonistic towards the UK's membership of the EU and have not engaged beyond the minimal requirements. Indeed, a former Head of the Civil Service,

Lord Butler, has told a Parliamentary Select Committee that he regards Brexit as a 'terrific opportunity' for the civil service.[33]

However, now that the civil service has to engage much more fully than ever before it will finally have some proper understanding of the EU's operational modes and of the policies that the UK government have agreed. Should the UK negotiate a relationship with the EU that is similar to that which persists through membership? The future relationship between the civil service and the EU could be different. It could be more engaged and better equipped to understand the differences between the different styles of operation that exist within a group of 27 or 28 countries and a state of four nations. If Scotland votes for independence, some of the understanding gained in these negotiations by civil servants may also inform any future relationships with Scotland and could inform the creation of a more federal structure of the UK. The civil service will also have to get to know the key officials in the European Commission and understand how they work in ways that have not troubled it before.

Another issue to consider is the extent to which the civil service has been competent in handling the relations between the EU and the UK in the past and how it stands up to the pressures of change. The pressure to work on Brexit comes at the time when the UK civil service is at its lowest staffing levels since 1945.

How will the UK respond to the Brexit deal?

The first issue to consider is whether there will be a Brexit deal negotiated as the result of triggering Article 50 or whether there will be a deal outside this process. If the government is prevented from invoking Article 50 through court and subsequent decisions, the EU may still offer the UK a revised package of arrangements that could

[33] Casalicchio, E. (2016) 'Lord Kerslake issues stark Brexit warning over civil service numbers', *Politics Home*, 22 November, www.politicshome.com/news/uk/government-and-public-sector/civil-service/operational-delivery/news/81041/lord-kerslake

deal with the free movement of labour. These changes may be offered to all member states by agreement as opening new treaty negotiations at a period of uncertainty may be considered to be too risky and time consuming.

Second, the UK government may invoke Article 50 but Parliament may limit its hand in negotiation and it may not be possible to find an agreement. In this case, the government may decide to attempt to revoke Article 50 or to agree with the EU to suspend it and continue as before or with some revised arrangements. Although the government may be able to invoke Article 50, it may not be able to leave the EEA without lengthy legal processes and therefore there would be no net benefits for the UK in leaving the EU.

A third scenario could occur where the economic position of the UK rapidly deteriorates and there are major effects on living standards. Although the economy appeared to be healthy and growing at the end of 2016, some final understanding that a full departure from the EU will happen, including from the single market, the free trade area and the customs union, could have a rapid and sharp effect on business confidence and investment. This could lead to firms leaving the UK and a failure to attract investment to replace what will be lost from the EIB. The UK has always been regarded as a safe and politically stable location for funds but may be replaced by other countries following what is seen as an unstable decision in the world markets. However, the uncertainties in the US may lead to the UK becoming more attractive for investors and a location for business. It is also uncertain whether the UK will be able to negotiate any new trade agreements with third countries following Brexit. There will also be a delay in the agreement of the 162 members in the WTO agreeing the terms of the UK's individual membership outside the EU. The UK may also find that Commonwealth countries will ally more with countries that are considered to be more powerful and also want trade arrangements with the EU in the same way as Canada.

The transitional exit from the EU may be agreed and initially appear to be favourable to business but the longer-term costs of uncertainty may undermine confidence. The UK will have to appoint many more civil servants to transpose and review EU legislation and also to devise new policies and legislation on those issues that the UK will be managing on its own, such as the application of new trade deals and climate change agreements.

The defence and security situation may change and there may be a renewal of cold war threats or new post cold war alliances between former foes. This might result in more incursions into EU member states. Given that the UK has not shown its support for EU member states by its actions following the referendum, EU member states may be less willing to assist the UK if there are threats made to its territories. The UK will also have little support from the US as it closes its military bases in the UK.

It is difficult to predict which of these many options, and as many more not yet thought of, might affect and influence the negotiations between the UK and EU. Assessing what the UK will look like beyond Brexit is difficult but this book has provided a framework for understanding what the influences, implications and outcomes of these negotiations might be in the coming months and years.

Index